Wishing on Your Own Star

Your Soul is Calling

By Alana Kay

Wishing on Your Own Star
Your Soul is Calling
Revised Edition

By Alana Kay
Published by Violet Phoenix Publishing
Maui, Hawaii
www.violetphoenixpublishing.com
Copyright 2017 by Alana Kay

ISBN 978-0-9727232-4-4

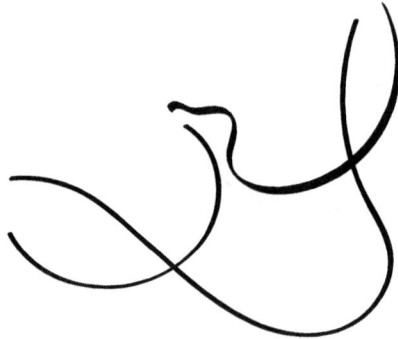

VIOLET PHOENIX PUBLISHING

Table of Contents

Preface

I have a weekly Internet radio program on Blogtalk Radio, where I do soul readings for my call in guests. Of the many intuitive gifts I have, the ability to see an individual's soul and to derive precise information from their voice is, I believe, the most valuable of my offerings to humanity. At the same time, I am not surprised when people express their inability to actualize those attributes and qualities I see in them. We live in a society that does not prioritize nor value self-actualization. To top it off, we see others through the blurry lenses we have developed through time.

I felt compelled to write *Wishing on Your Own Star* to address this complex human dilemma. The spiritual movement has opened the doors to address this, but I feel the need to deepen the search for the soul and help people use this connection to harmonize humanity.

Society in general has given us a set of rules that are failing miserably. The purpose of the spiritual movement has been to start a new dialog. This book has loads of dialog to quell the inquisitive and confused mind. Even if you have studied and practiced spiritual modalities in your life, there will be many things herein that will help solidify the thought processes necessary to rise to your highest level of attainment.

Recently someone expressed that it is not possible to teach a person how to live with their heart (soul) through a book. There is some truth to that. While there is nothing better than being in the presence of a facilitator who is aligned with Source energy to guide your way – kind of like a soul Sherpa, we don't always have someone available to guide us so I have spent years figuring out how I will explain these things to people so they can go through their transformation in their own way and in their own time – with or without the help of a soul Sherpa.

I can provide the how, but it will be up to you to do the work. You will have to change how you perceive your self and others in order to rise.

Spiritualists refer to our distorted perception of the world and others as projection. I have discovered that we are only able to see into others to the extent of the depths we have reached inside of our own being. That is why, in order to heal the world, we must begin with our self.

I am not saying we should stand by and allow others to abuse or mistreat us, I am saying that we need to begin humanity's ascent by understanding that humans behaving badly is born of being disconnected from our souls and God. I am on Facebook several times a day and believe me – I believe there is enough shaming going around to kill us all.

We are suffering on both the personal and group level because of this programming – or karmic history. The problems in our world will be solved when each individual takes responsibility for correcting their spiritual perception. We help countless others when we raise our individual vibration because we are all connected.

We only have two modes – connected to our soul or disconnected to our soul. Our ability to reach Peace on Earth is contingent upon our ability to recognize the difference. In order to unwind this huge misstep we have all taken part in creating, we will need large doses of forgiveness for ourselves and for others.

I was raised as many people are. Parents are too busy, wounded and dealing with their own issues – strapped with a litany of survival challenges in a world where it has become every person for his or her self. We used to be supported by tribes and everybody had their role. Life was simpler and our expectations of our selves and our lives were simpler. It is different now. People are not happy with the status quo and the spiritual movement is prompting us to listen to that still small voice that lives inside of all of us.

Most of us don't want to be a part of a tribe any-more, but we also have become very stressed out by the dog-eat-dog mentality that individualism has wrought. Underneath all of this, there is harmony and it lies in the unified field, where all of our soul perspectives are in harmony, while remaining vastly unique. In order for this dream to manifest, we must become aligned with our souls.

I think one of the most significant, powerful quota-tions from a spiritual teacher in recent time is one by Marianne Williamson:

"Our deepest fear is not that we are inadequate. Our deepest fear is that we are powerful beyond mea-sure. It is our light, not our darkness that most fright-ens us. We ask ourselves, Who am I to be brilliant, gorgeous, talented, fabulous? Actually, who are you *not* to be? You are a child of God. Your playing small does not serve the world. There is nothing enlight-ened about shrinking so that other people won't feel insecure around you. We are all meant to shine, as children do. We were born to make manifest the glo-ry of God that is within us. It's not just in some of us; it's in everyone. And as we let our own light shine, we unconsciously give other people permission to do the same. As we are liberated from our own fear, our presence automatically liberates others."

One time when a woman caller was expressing her doubt about that which I saw in her while spirit was urging me to recommend that she work on self-love, I said, "If you saw you the way I see you, you would love you too." That pretty much says it all. We are all brilliant, creative, loving beings, but we have not been raised or groomed to be in alignment to that awareness. We have not been taught how to know who we truly are and to embrace our uniqueness.

I have always been a positive person and have always been able to find the silver lining in any person or circumstance. I think we are born with a propensity to be either negative or positive. It is time to start listening to the positive people!! That said, I also have always been able to look deeply into people – all people and see their beautiful soul. I am sharing decades of knowledge and insights for readers in Wishing on Your Own Star because it is my wish that you will be encouraged to embark your climb and to know the Heaven that dwells within.

This is the meaning of self Love. It is not self-aggrandizement; it is an awareness that allows you know who you are on the deepest levels and to live in full acceptance and expression of that energy.

I think sometimes people believe it would be too much work and that they are better off just avoiding the urgings of the inner self. Unfortunately, we are either rising or we are falling. That is the way energy is set up.

I have always believed in Heaven on Earth. I had epiphanies about this when I was a child. In 1994, I was living in Milwaukee, Wisconsin where the crime rate was out of hand. I had just made it through another grey winter with a miserable, verbally abusive spouse along with series of events in my life led me to a state of exasperation. Practically on bended knee, I asked Spirit/God/Source, what do you want me to do with my life? A headache that persisted for most of my life with a severe increase in intensity evaporated from my head the instant I uttered the last word of this life-changing question.

I was led through a series of events that could only be referred to as magical and so well orchestrated that there was no question that I was in the throws of a divine intervention. Not only had my angels entered my life, but I was about to embark on a long journey back to the center of my being – a return to my authentic self. This ascent is available to everybody and there are metaphysical laws that will direct the process.

To know thy self is to know Heaven.

We live in a vibrational Universe where everything is connected through quantum entanglement. The numbers of stars, planets and galaxies defy comprehension to our human psyches, yet as incarnate humans, we are well aware of the miniscule, seemingly insignificant part that we are entirely responsible for - our own life, our own self, our own path. And yet, because of quantum entanglement, each of us is as integral as creation itself.

We arrive on this planet at our own chosen time and in our own way. We set out with dogged determination, chasing after things and working out problems, kick up a bunch of dust and then we leave when it is our time to depart. There is nothing of this solid reality that we will take with us to the other realms, yet our experience here is so darn serious and as many have discovered - inescapable. We can't kill our spirit, though many have tried. When an individual gets tired of trying to quiet their soul, they surrender.

We are spirits having a physical experience on a planet that is constantly evolving. With so much going on, how is it possible to walk our own sacred journey? With a consciousness shift going on at this juncture in our evolution, the chaos is almost unbearable. Yet, many have heard the call and felt the prompting to come back to integrity and don't know where to begin. Living a chaotic, inauthentic life has become unbearable and the changes that are necessary to ascend can make the soul searcher a bit fearful.

There is only one way to go now and that is up – or as spirit would have it – within. Dedication and persistence are key during this critical time of awakening of the human spirit. I wish it were easier than this, but remember, you signed up for this. Just imagine – if you signed up for this, you must be pretty amazing.

Does all of this sound selfish or self-serving? Haven't we been taught not to toot our own horn? What if you knew that most of us who are walking around this planet are functioning at perhaps only 10% of our true capacity? Since we are all connected through quantum entanglement – it appears energetically that we are all a bunch of drowning people pulling each other down – deeper and deeper into despair. The question remains – do we want to be victims or do we want to do what we need to do to rise individually and collectively and become the great beings we are destined to be?

Perhaps you have tried to be your best self and perhaps you know what that feels like. Most likely you remember a time or a day when you felt absolutely connected to all that is grand and good. If you gave up your climb because the weight of every day life and every day people became too much to bear, you are not alone. Especially now, it takes special tools to rise above the fray. And when you do, you take countless others with you because you are no longer projecting lower vibrating energy outward for others to absorb.

When we shrink, we take others down with us. When we rise we take people up with us.

Our individual and group ascent over the next couple decades will seem a bit like a frog jumping up the well, so to speak. Sometimes we will have two leaps forward and one leap back. Hang in there because this is inescapable. It is why we are here. We have to get through this time period and every bit of progress we make personally serves all of humanity and will continue to lay the pathways for the generations to come.

Chapter One
The Struggle is Real

Whenever I look out on the nighttime sky, I become completely enraptured with the power and beauty of the stars. I have often found the starlight to be one of the most centering and powerful forces available when I need clarity. It is said that each star is the dwelling place of the individual units of consciousness or the storehouse for our causal body's energy. I believe this to be true and I am sure that this is why we are so enamored with stars. It is as though we are reminded of the magnanimity of life in its purest state when we gaze up at them. It also helps to put the little things back into the proper perspective.

Just as the starlight endures, the consciousness that dwells within all of us has always been and will never cease to exist. Beginnings and endings are part of the physical world, which has been co-created with this same energy. The Love and life that we feel inside our hearts goes with us into any dimension we enter. It is our soul that directs our undertakings and the physical body is simply a vehicle or a temporary disposition.

This consciousness, which may be referred to as our over-soul or higher self, has been through an evolution that is for the most part, something that we cannot accurately fathom and this is probably the main reason that we often do not remember too much from our past lives. Some believe that our individual units of consciousness were involved in the creation of our planet and that we have incarnated as beings other than human throughout Earth's evolution, seeing it through the many phases it has gone through to come to fruition as a life supporting planet. We needed to participate in the successful completion of our planet before we could begin our human evolution. Although it does not always seem like it, there is a reason for all of our lives and all of the drama throughout human history.

Even the simplest of esoteric belief systems acknowledge that we have had at least several incarnations as a human being. Some believe we have had tens of thousands of incarnations, while *A Course in Miracles* states that there aren't really past lives because there is only this moment in time. I realize that in the truest sense, our I AM presence is the only true presence, but for the purpose of working with energy and clearing programming, it may be necessary to take past life experiences into account. Now that is some serious food for thought! It is possible to embrace paradoxes.

Regardless of our beliefs, spirit makes sure that we know everything we need to know for this lifetime as long as we are open to it. I mention the subject because it helps to open this door should some out of the ordinary things occur. The ability to access on a need to know basis is part of present moment awareness.

As we move through life and our evolutionary spiral, our higher self makes sure we have everything we need and every thing we need to know.

I don't believe we have to intimately understand the grandeur and history of our soul, but we do need to have a healthy respect for it as well as a general overview of its blueprint, since we all bring our special imprint to the table and should honor and cherish those aspects. Most of us are aware from a young age what our particular talents and likes and dislikes are. It is important to be familiar with our soul lineage because it serves as our support system on the other side. As we get more familiar with our particular contribution and the wisdom we have accumulated throughout our individual evolution, we then learn how to apply it to this lifetime, in this body, on planet Earth.

Our higher self is that part of our identity that is really in charge of things in our lives and it knows quite a bit more than our earthly selves. It knows our history both in this lifetime as well as our previous lifetimes. It knows and understands the goals that were set forth upon our current incarnation. For most of us, there are many roads we need to walk down and many choices to make along the way. For these reasons, it is wise to learn to let it lead us. Surrendering to our soul is a practiced discipline. We surrender and feel the flow and then we get off track again. It is up to us to continually make the right choices.

Even if we make mistakes and end up taking detour routes, all we need to do is correct our path and get back on the path of our soul which has been and always will be aligned with eternity – untouched and shining a light for us.

We could think of our soul as an external hard drive. Our higher self is the voice of wisdom that speaks to us as well as the creator of the visions we receive. When we talk about surrender, this is what we mean – we surrender to our higher self instead of letting our small self lead the way. If we learn to allow our higher self to lead us, step by step, it is impossible to go astray. Our soul is always one step ahead of us, but does not always follow a predictable or straight pathway, as our logical mind would have it be. As we learn to trust this energy, we develop what is known as faith. We let go of the toiling of the ego mind and feel our gentle, powerful soul go out before us. There is great peace in the feeling of being protected and led by our Source energy.

We need to slow down in order to be led by our soul.

Although we are here to have a good time, we are also here to take on certain challenges and we will be guided to learn much. Very often, we are involved in something that our ego is judging as yucky, yet our big self knows that it is for our own good. Whenever we find our thoughts and feelings bouncing around, sometimes being entirely contradictory – it is most likely that we are volleying between our heart and our head as well as many other forces. In time we learn who the winner is. We actually move more quickly through seeming difficulties if we surrender to the moment and do our best and then some.

Our full over-soul/higher self has much too much energy to fit into our physical body and this too varies by individual. While we long for our purpose, we also long for our soul's energy. Almost all cravings are the ego's yearning for union with the energy of the soul. There are stories of those who had near death experiences and whence rejoining with the larger self, a part of them did not want to return to their relatively mundane earthly existences. To their dismay, a force pushed them back into their earthbound body because they were not finished. It is the soul of the individual and the Angel guides that are responsible for this push back into the physical body because they know that the individual journey is not complete. The physical and spiritual bodies have a mutual need for each other and are designed to function together in lock step. It is critical to become acutely aware of how all of our bodies feel, so that we become adept at fine-tuning our alignment. We should know what alignment feels like even if it eludes us.

While a part of us yearns for the other side, our carnal being clings desperately to physical life by grand design because this instinct protects us from being lackadaisical about our existence here. Without this mechanism, we would likely become complacent. The cycle of death, integration and incarnation is a long and detailed process and the larger part of our selves knows that it is true! We get impatient waiting in line at the grocery store; imagine how spirit feels about us having to recycle in order to complete soul goals. Premature death short circuits the evolutionary path of the soul and is also the reason that murder and suicide are such big karmic no no's.

Spiritual disciplines, spiritual practices and self-counseling help to quell the physical aspects of our being.

Although the bliss we experience upon rejoining with the energy of the other side is alluring, extremely comfortable levels of bliss may be obtained on Earth as well if we learn how to maintain the state of being fully integrated with our spirit. Getting to know this energy that resides in us is a multi-faceted endeavor that begins by beginning to honor our instincts and feelings. We do this primarily by tuning into our instincts and acting thereupon. The more we expose ourselves to our soul, the more familiar it becomes. The only reason that we don't feel bliss is that we have lost our connection.

Our physical body only feels good when it is energetically clear and connected to our soul Source energy.

We should feel healthy, energetically brilliant and deeply content at all times. This would be the case if we had all of our cosmic energy flowing through our bodies at all times. I know this sounds like a very high level of achievement, and indeed it is, but I am laying it out as the ultimate goal –taking priority over other goals that we have been taught to value, such as financial, social status and others.

As humans, we can increase this energy by drawing more of it in to our bodies and also by using it in our lives. In common terms, this energy is known as charisma. Why do some of us have access to this charisma or life force, while others do not? To begin with, our over-soul energy storehouse is increased by the positive use of our life force throughout our individual evolution.

Some of the factors involved in building our energy cache include accepting responsibility for its proper application and use, while using it for the benefit of the advancement of humanity. While on Earth, the more we are tapped into the creative force, the greater our light, and the greater our power and responsibility.

Very often, some people who came into this life with plenty of charisma did not understand their power and ended up misusing it. Because it is so tempting, if one is not careful, the misuse of power for egotistical means can result in self-destruction. While having more charisma has its benefits, it is also easier to spin out of control. We don't want to shy away from charisma simply because we have seen some people misuse it. Because we have not been educated on how to use our power, some people mistakenly believe it is easier to follow others, dim their light, or numb themselves with addictive substances. It takes work and constant refinement to build and balance this power.

In the new paradigm it will be increasingly important to arrive at new ways of looking at power

Soul Searching...

Elvis Presley struggled with his, Michael Jackson couldn't contain his, Shirley McLain explored hers, Oprah has shared hers, and Betty White does a great job of aligning with hers while some people feel that they have lost theirs. One thing is certain: we all have a soul. It is the power that energizes us, animates us and directs us while we are in these human bodies on planet Earth, yet, we cannot adopt someone else's path or someone else's essence, we must learn to honor our own unique blueprint. If we don't like ourselves or wish we were someone else, chances are, we don't know what we are made of and who we were truly meant to be. Our bodies are designed specifically to house our individual soul blueprints and it is only misalignment that causes discomfort and distress.

Because each of us is at a different point of development, we will always encounter different choices as we go. Deep down inside, we may be the next Elvis or Oprah, but our placement on the spiral dictates that we become the best house painter or furniture salesman we can be first. It is good for us to know if we are hanging on to mundane things because we are afraid of the risks involved in reaching higher or if we are not ready to leap yet because there is more to learn. Knowing ourselves intimately and having a good intuitive counselor helps with this.

As important as it is to be in touch with our soul, we often find it to be elusive. How many of us know how our soul feels? Maybe you have met yours when you felt love or passion. Maybe you have met your soul in moments of silence. Perhaps you've met your soul when your back was against the wall and you suddenly pulled out a moment of genius or strength you never knew you had. I am pretty certain that you would not be reading this book if you had never experienced a time when you felt truly connected to your greater self. We need to remember the times when we felt aligned to Source energy because these memories help us to get re-centered when we are feeling off.

In order to demonstrate that we have distinct and palpable blueprints, people have conducted experiments where long time partners were blindfolded and challenged to identify their mate from a lineup. This is a very interesting concept and would probably make a great learning tool for workshops.

In our search for the inner light, we meditate, take yoga classes, read spiritual literature, attend church or consult oracles. We have heard gurus and religious zealots say that the true self is realized when all attachment to things of this world are relinquished.

The main focus of teachings of the Kabbalah, which was kept hidden in earlier centuries, is focusing on becoming one with God. The truth is that there is value in all of these vehicles and we learn which ones work best for us as we go. We may make use of the wisdom of many spiritual philosophies and modalities as well as personally devised or borrowed affirmations to keep us in line.

All spiritual modalities should emphasize going within. Choose what works for you. If someone says they are your master or you should obey them, it is not a legitimate spiritual path.

Even those who know full well how to quiet their monkey mind and listen to the still small voice have trouble getting there and staying there at times. Just like anything else on earth, there are some undeniable natural laws that come into play, and there are individual choices that may be used to enhance them.

We need to live with Love, clarity and soul alignment in order to experience Heaven on Earth. This state has nothing to do with our surroundings. Some of us may find ourselves surrounded by sheer horror and despair and have no other choice but to see whatever light we can. I have heard of prisoners of war telling stories of the inconceivable acts that they were witnessing. They said that the only way they were able to stay sane was to forgive their captors. Some of us have trouble forgiving even the slightest of human missteps. We can make these choices despite that which we find ourselves surrounded by as well as that which we have previously experienced and are still carrying around with us. Achieving a state of Heaven on Earth is also called ascension and almost everybody who is incarnated at this time is programmed to ascend!

Alignment with our soul gives us clear inner guidance, creativity, health, peace, joy and satisfaction.

We have created a society that is very enamored with the thrill of being entertained. Concerts, sporting events and movie theatres are big business and big draws for consumers because we need to be entertained. For many of us, ordinary life can be very lackluster, so we seek that which is outside of us – enjoying events that seem larger than life at times. Wouldn't it be nice to live like a child again, excited about each new day and all the adventure life brings? If this were the case, we would not have to seek so much of what is outside of us in order to feel alive.

One of the main reasons for fatigue is lack of alignment with Source energy. Our soul gives us energy for the things it wants us to do. When we block out our inner guidance, we essentially block out our life force energy.

Creative people of all kinds - painters, writers, performing artists know that they need to be in a certain place inside themselves in order to create or more definitively speaking, co-create with Source to produce something that others will enjoy or pay good money for. We love our entertainers and artists because they take us to a better place when we enjoy their work. In effect, they act as something of a placeholder for the cosmos and often have the power to bring us back to the fold.

Although we place artists and entertainers on a pedestal, we also have the ability to access the creative portal, which is the same as our instinctive center - our seat of wisdom. We all have different reasons to access the creative portal, whether it is as an entertainer or artist, or any other task in life. It is a matter of spending time there and seeing what develops on an individual level. Even if we don't have much time to explore this side of life, we can start by using what little time we have.

Even if we are not destined to be an artist or performer, it is possible to use this same portal to navigate the things of life, to communicate and to make good decisions. When we first begin to use intuition and instincts to guide us, we have to be careful to also learn discernment or we may jump to improper conclusions about the information or instructions we believe we are receiving. It is wise to take things slowly and learn to discern energy signatures and fields of consciousness, topics that are covered in subsequent chapters. Discerning these things is ultra important skill refinement involved in gaining useful guidance. Only that which comes from a higher source is truly valuable.

Remember as a youngster, being in school and wanting to play and explore? Our inner instincts were trying to direct us, yet we were told to ignore them and to pay attention to the books and the blackboard. We were taught by authoritative people at a very young age to ignore our instincts and that our worth was defined by our ability to submit to the authorities - the authorities outside of us, not the authority that dwelled within us. This is the primary reason we have produced a world full of sheep-like people who believe all the media hype instead of a world full of strong, empowered, self-starting, self-sufficient people. People lose sight of their inner power when they buy into the bad habits of the herd.

When it comes to education, we have been teaching children the same way since the industrial revolution when we needed to train little robots to work in factories. I'd like to see people rise up and fulfill their purpose in designing new education systems that will instill values and presence of mind in our brilliant indigo and crystal children.

Because we have been so trained away from the awareness of our soul and our inner guidance, it will take time and patience, both individually and as a group, to learn a new way of living. Rebirthing is a step-by-step process. I believe that where we go wrong in our thinking regarding the concepts of intuition and creativity is that we tend to believe that either you have it or you don't have it. This just is not so. With the right tools, anybody can become aligned and clear. This requires a state of allowing because we are designed to be intuitive and creative. Most of the time, we just need to get out of our own way.

In the process of re-birthing, we begin by recapturing the enthusiasm, curiosity and joy of our youth. We need to nurture the child within and take this precious being with us wherever we go. We need to forgive those who imprinted on us because they did not know any better. They were busy dealing with their own issues and doing the best they could. Carrying around blame will only hurt us in the end anyway.

We have a tendency to lose our patience or believe that we are doing something wrong if we don't get it fast enough or if we have to keep getting back on the horse. We have to practice forgiving our selves and others, but we also need to improve our ability to take responsibility for our part and not hang on too long. With this set of psychological tools in tow, we strengthen our ability to evolve. Esther Hicks, who channels the teachings of Abraham says, "You will never get it done, and you will never get it wrong." This does not mean we make endless excuses for hovering in the sludge, but it puts life in a more workable perspective.

Letting go of judgment will create a clearer state of mind and improve perceptive ability as well as enhance spirit communication

Because each human soul is on a course of evolution that is much like a spiral, it is difficult to know where one really is in their climb. One may have a nice home and a great job and be very materially focused, while another may have great creative abilities while struggling financially. These two people may be entirely equal in their evolution if the souls of both of the individuals are engaged in a path that will balance the physical and the creative. The materially successful one will encounter life events that open up their center, while the creative one's endeavors will eventually bear fruit, gaining recognition and financial rewards for their work.

In order to circumvent the drama involved in competition and power struggles, our primary focus needs to be on getting to know ourselves while trusting others to handle their own path. Unless we have access to very detailed, historical information in regard to a certain individual, we will most likely misjudge them. Additionally, those involved in families of varying sizes often encounter difficulty when the individuals choose to embark on a course of self-discovery. In order for us to move neatly into our next cycle as humans, we need to get accustomed to letting go of each other while gaining higher levels of security within ourselves.

In the level of consciousness known as the Akashic records, there is a history of all of the evolutionary data about each being. In the absence of Christ Consciousness, we will always see people from our own limited perspective, but the Angels and the Masters see things through the lens of pure unconditional Love and have ready access to the Akashic records. The teachings of Abraham's law of allowing has its roots in the understanding of the spiritual nature of individualized curricula and the power of releasing people to their own path of attainment-trusting the energy to land them safely back home – the same destination we all seek in our heart of hearts.

As a spiritual medium, many people come to me with a list of questions about other people. We need to get more focused on our own piece of the puzzle because it is the only one we are in control of. People will not leave us just because we have untangled ourselves and as a matter of fact, hanging more loosely will provide for more joyful relationships. If people are meant to be in our lives, they will be.

The extent to which we have lost touch with our inner self varies by individual as well. It really depends on the influence that parents, teachers and peers have had on our individual personality type. Becoming intimately familiar with how the people and experiences of our lives have imprinted our personality and our energy as well as how we have allowed these events to either create discordant energy or help us evolve, is a step by step, one day at a time proposition and it does not happen over night. When we break down and analyze the dynamics of our psychological and spiritual development, we remap our past and redirect our destiny. Not all spiritual teachers agree with this, however. It is up to the individual to decide what works for them.

Some people are more affected and manipulated than others and outer influence affects each person in a different way. We all come into each incarnation with a set of highly personalized and complex issues to work through based on our life history, soul goals and astrological influences. For this reason, I believe it is good to get really familiar with our personality type and our triggers. With the goal of being on center as the ideal, we can work to see what is causing us to lose track of our place of wisdom and power as we go through our days - and why. Journaling helps to identify our vulnerabilities.

Sometimes the drama and chaos flies at us so quickly that it is difficult to sort it all out. We will have to forgive ourselves over and over. Once we get the past sorted out, then we have to make sure we reflect daily on issues that make us uncomfortable, and get things sorted out so that we don't get the system clogged up again.

"The intuitive mind is a sacred gift and the rational mind is a faithful servant. We have created a society that honors the servant and has forgotten the gift." Albert Einstein

Getting back in touch with the instinctive self…

Modern life has caused us to become too physically focused for our own good. Much of what we have become is the result of herd mentality and cookie cutter identities. While we are good at being part of the herd, we have lost touch with our true identities. From a metaphysical viewpoint, we are ungrounded and disconnected. These factors are the cause of the malaise in the world today. If we can learn how to be true to our selves and align with our paths, we will live in peace and harmony with each other and the Earth. Inner harmony and alignment create the state of energetic integrity.

The energetic world or the unseen part of life functions under a different set of laws than those of the kinetic world and this is one of the main reasons we have difficulty integrating the two. This is not to say that while we are on a spiritual trek, we should avoid or disregard physical laws. It simply means that we need to take a closer look at the undercurrents of life and how they relate to physical outcomes. The road to perfect integration begins with understanding that true power and clarity lies in the ability to allow the spiritual to drive the physical. The physical cannot drive the spiritual, so the spiritual will always win in the end. It is much easier to follow our spirit to begin with.

At times, the fear of the unseen or the unknown prevents us from making healthy changes. There is so much beauty and magic in the world and within each of our hearts. In order to look deeper into our soul, we must be comfortable with feeling deeper. For instance, if we are aloof when we really want to express Love, we clog up our feeling mechanisms. Continuing to withhold or mask our real feelings creates blockages and eventually causes illnesses. Avoiding our depth also reduces our capacity for joy and our ability to use our instinctive center for intuition. In effect, we distance ourselves from our true being when we avoid our feelings. This pertains to all feelings – whether they are loss, Love, laughter or anger. If we handle them properly, they do not have jagged edges nor do they wax and wane. Our juices are flowing like a beautiful, life-giving river at all times and under all circumstances. There is great power in this knowledge.

While we should not stay in a state of pain, sadness or anger long enough to brood over it, we need to go there if we are feeling it and deal with the issues related to the pain. We should rise out of the state with a refreshed feeling of exuberance and a new viewpoint, if we have dealt with the lessons involved in the highest manner. These things teach us about our self, our imprinting and our history. As we become clearer in our feeling center, we become stronger in our instincts, creativity and guidance.

If we allow our feelings to take us into the depths of our being, they will walk us right into a greater place of wisdom and then propel us on to the next level of existence – only if we allow them to. Very often, when we go deep, we begin to cry. So often we are tempted to stop ourselves because it feels too raw and we have a tendency to feel silly. We have not been taught that the act of crying and expressing tears takes us to a better place and we need to embrace this and see it as strength now, instead of seeing it as a weakness.

When we initially go inside, we will find everything that we have put there throughout our lifetime. This can be a bit of a Pandora's box. We may find things we didn't even know we stuffed down. The thing is, if we stuff things and don't process them in the highest spiritual fashion, we will be acting out in ways that we may not be too proud of and encountering turmoil in our relationships, becoming jaded. Additionally, we will continue to attract the same old circumstances over and over as a result, we end up ingraining our experiences into our chemistry and adopting them as our identity. It is much better to re-write our story and chalk things up to lessons learned, effectively taking a step up the evolutionary ladder.

I once heard the story of a woman who quit drinking and ended up crying for an entire year, all the while releasing the hurt that she had accumulated over years of denial. There was just too much stuffed down for her to process everything, so the crying did the large part of the releasing for her. Nonetheless, she did need to go through the process in order to heal. Crying is actually a very good practice as long as we don't go into self-pity. It is a valuable tool for releasing pent up feelings. Through this process, we also re-sort and re-file events of our lives. Ultimately, crying is the opening of the soul and is not always related to sadness.

Crying is one of the most common manifestations of going deep into the heart chakra.

Fully embracing and expressing our feelings does not mean taking others down in the process, blaming or becoming destructive to our selves or others. It means that we need to get comfortable with going deep and finding out what is really in there or what is blocking the good feeling stuff. This is something that should be done between our selves and God or a very good counselor or friend. After clearing out the feeling center, we need to allow time for integration. After a period of integration, we begin to notice changes in our lives.

If we have allowed ourselves to feel love, express our selves, cry and dream; we will have imbued ourselves with a much greater capacity for creativity on all levels because these acts of human nature create a well that is deep and wide. The feeling center needs to be clear in addition to being large. If we are carrying around pain and blame, then we have allowed our experiences to rob us of our clarity and peace, and we have diminished power to create.

One of the reasons that highly creative and unusual people sometimes come across as a bit crazy is that it has not been the norm to learn to practice the art of bringing to Earth the unmanifested, while keeping all planes of existence into a balanced state. As a result, we find it difficult to be connected and also function in the world of form. This lack of development is an attribute of the larger group mentality, while there are those who have figured out how to be the eccentric while walking among the flock. It can be tricky and I invite more of those who have creative urges and a desire to blossom from a soul level to come out and play. Let's get better at accepting each other's individuality and eccentricity. If we do so, it would be of great help to all of humanity.

In the Golden Age, more people will embrace their inner gifts and we will have more stars and less super stars.

The good news is that we can heal any thing that we find in there with the right spiritual tools. I must say, this is one of the things that I love about the new age-we have brought about new ways of restoring purity to our lives and learning to live again in very positive ways.

Our feelings are the gateway to our soul. Our soul fills up our body by sending our life force throughout our energy centers. Our body is intended to be an out-picturing of our soul, and the energy centers represent different parts of expression and thought. We develop these energy centers throughout our lives by the input we allow and the thoughts and feelings we express. This is one of the reasons that people have such unique appearances, even identical twins. This concept is the fabric of some healing modalities that recognize the symbolism and interconnectedness of the parts of the human body.

Obtaining true alignment with our soul energy guarantees a certain level of health as a result.

That said, a person who avoids their feelings, stuffing them down or internalizing them in a negative fashion often develops heart or digestive problems because these behaviors affect the heart chakra, solar plexus chakra and related energy pathways. All discordant energy creates energy blockages in the region of the body where the carnal mind is out of synch with the soul. Because the soul has God-like characteristics, it cannot fit into a vessel that is riddled with discordant energy. When we are loaded up with blockages, we lose the connection to our instincts and intuition and ultimately our health as well.

If we accept the things that come into our lives as learning tools that are specially designed to advance and enhance our personal evolutionary curriculum, we will then process things in a more spiritually healthy manner. Events that we judge as seemingly difficult or insurmountable are likely to be our best teachers and our greatest gifts. In the book, Bringer's of the Dawn, author Barbara Marciniak makes one of the most brilliant references to this concept that I have ever heard: "It is like the Universe is dumping gold on the lawn and we are complaining that it is ruining the grass."

We have to learn how to follow and honor the energy that is moving us through our lives if we want things to improve. Because our soul is in charge, it will provide us with more energy for the goals it has laid out. Sometimes fatigue is attributable to the fact that we have shut our self off from Source by ignoring our soul. When we ignore our soul, we close ourselves off to our supply of universal energy.

By now it should be clear that while the cookie-cutter life used to be the ultimate goal or the American dream, in the future, insofar as spiritual goals are designed, it is not. A generic blueprint does not teach us anything of value. The ultimate goal is to fulfill one's unique destiny.

Connecting to our soul is a learned discipline. Because it is easy to get distracted, we need to commit to a spiritual practice of any kind that works for us, and discipline ourselves to stick to it. It is up to us to make the decision. For the most part, spirit is not going to drop down in front of us and hit us over the head to try to get our attention, although it sometimes does so and it usually is not pleasant when it happens this way.

I have heard many stories of people who were so distracted by a frantic life and endless list of things to do that they found themselves getting caught up in the rushing around, bickering, frustration and anger that ensues – only to be awakened by a tragic error that would not have occurred if they had been focused and centered. This is also what causes people to forget their children in cars while they dash off to the office. I know of at least two people who suffered permanent damage and or inadvertently killed loved ones because they let a fit of rage get the best of them. These events are horrible, but indicative of the lifestyles many of us have adopted. We do not have to learn through tragedy or near death experiences. We will learn and it is pretty much up to us how we will learn. How will you choose?

Developing our awareness of spirit and receiving the strength and the gifts that the energetic world brings to us requires time, dedication, discipline and patience. It is a building process, much like learning in a class or building muscles. Staying connected to spirit may or may not be automatic, depending on the individual. It also requires a great deal of letting go and open-mindedness because it will present us with entirely new experiences and thoughts as we go.

Having our consciousness nestled deep within our bodies, grounded and centered in spiritual light, is the place that Esther Hicks is talking about when she is referring to the Vortex, but this can only occur and become an easy space to maintain when we become familiar and comfortable with it. This means we need to seek it, embrace it and spend time with it in order to get comfortably familiar.

The instinctive center or feeling center is the communication vortex between our soul and our bodies and is like a vessel that we either neglect or make good use of. It could also be viewed as a spiritual muscle. The more we use it, the larger and stronger it becomes. When people begin a spiritual journey, they are often instructed to learn how to be still and go within. This can be confusing to those who are not accustomed to focusing their attention on their inner being because we are trained to be outwardly focused, easily responding to this stimuli from years of exposure and repetition.

We can learn to respond instinctively once again, through practice and dedication, while unlearning the practice of internalizing the outside world. Spirituality is the process of learning to come from the inside – out. When we learn to respond to our instincts, we begin to take right action (or refrain from action) in regard to life's events instead of creating more karma. This may also be referred to as tapping into the un-manifested.

Tuning into our clear inner guidance is key to walking and following our unique path. Everybody knows his or her self to a certain extent. I have met some people who tell me that they have no talent or creative ability whatsoever. Some people, on the other hand, were blessed enough to have parents who spotted their talents and put them in special schools from a very young age. I always encourage people to do the things they love even if they are not going to develop them as a profession. The things we love to dabble in are very important for staying aligned with our spirit presence.

In addition to enjoying activities that sing to our heart, there are the little things we love. We need to develop healthy habits around creating sacred space. Sacred space may include anything from the jewelry we wear to making our house a relaxing haven. Most really wealthy and successful people are very good at tending to their bodies and their space –nurturing habits that serve to keep our lights shining in the cacophony of the world that surrounds us and often threatens to consume us. When it comes to attracting our desired circumstances, we must begin by demonstrating to the Universe that which we want. Starting small is better than not starting at all.

We must also have our quiet and our still time and learn to enjoy having nothing to think about and nothing to do. I have heard people say that they have tried meditating and nothing comes to them. This is because we have to learn how to be still and focus on our center for a long period of time before it is ready to begin processing information for us. To begin to receive inner guidance without the discipline of stillness is the same as a beginner driving a car too quickly – the driver would easily loose control. At times our soul puts us in a void simply because our body or mind needs rest. We need to embrace this concept in order to become efficient, effective and energetic. I am one of those who have had to really get disciplined at appreciating down time and silence.

This too becomes a learning process as we learn to understand the language interaction between our earthly self and our spirit self. Also, if there is pain, blockage or clutter there, it must be healed by talking it out either internally or externally and going through a forgiveness process or by crying and releasing. Stored up blockages can keep us from enjoying the stillness of the moment. There are many books regarding the process of healing and many practitioners of different modalities versed in this art, but there are some general and easy to use practices that should help clear blocked energy. Intentional breathing, prayer, yoga, energy clearing exercises, expressing, journaling and color therapy are readily available at any given time to most individuals.

Sweeping in front of our own door is how we heal the world - one soul at a time.

The stress of the world is simply the clashing of egos. Imagine how life would flow and thrive if everybody was acting and functioning from a place of spiritual integrity and purity. Heaven is ours for the asking and the nice thing about this is that we don't have to wait for others to do it. We can achieve a state of flow and synchronicity even if others don't seem to be on the same page as us.

Laws of metaphysics dictate that all things must conform to the highest vibration available. Therefore, because being soul centered carries a high vibratory frequency, it will cause others to raise their vibration as well. This is something we all must know. We do not exist in a void.

I would like to emphasize that if we rely on certain people to help bring us back to center, we may want to wean ourselves of this habit because the people we rely on for strength will inevitably become unavailable and this is too great a responsibility to put on somebody else anyway. People relying on another to make them happy or bring them back to their moorings is one of the most destructive forces a relationship can endure, and unfortunately this has been the norm in the old paradigm. When people cling to each other, the issues of co-dependency rear their ugly head and life becomes a battle. True power lies in knowing that we carry this strength with us at all times and it is spiritually healthier to allow ourselves and others to evolve freely.

If we each dedicate our days to beginning and ending in our hearts and focusing on the growth of our soul and allow others to do the same, we will be doing the greatest service that we can do for humanity and the benefits will be tremendous.

Chapter Two
The 1000 Day Climb

Motivational speakers and authors such as Wayne Dyer, Tony Robbins and Louise Hay have written books and charged us up through speaking and presentations that leave us wanting more, yet we find ourselves returning to our old ways more often than not.

The reasons for the difficulty in actuating change are many. First of all, we exist on many intertwined levels. We have our mental, physical, spiritual and emotional bodies. You could say there are even more levels of self, but this should be enough to get started. Within each of these bodies, there are cellular memories, habits, engrained imprinting and even programming running the gamut from etheric to physical information. We have all of this, notwithstanding our DNA and quantum entanglement with our birth families and countless others.

It takes time to remove the old programming and replace it with new. One reason people have said,

"Fake it until you make it" is that we need to actually experience a change in order to reprogram our data banks. Introducing high vibrations to an energy system flushes out the old, but it is up to us to create the new.

Neurogenesis is the process of creating new nerve connections in the physical body including the brain. While studies are still progressing, the gist of it is that there is now confirmation that we *do* form new neurons and neural connections even into late adulthood and that we are indeed able to do something about it. It was once thought that there was an acceleration of growth only in the tender years, with a continual degradation of neurons and neuron connections from there. It slows down, but it does not degrade unless we engage in destructive behavior.

It has also been determined that our DNA is not static.

While growth slows as time goes on (all of that nerve growth is not necessary after the basic framework is laid), each person's individual experience will very significantly. It has been recently confirmed that new experiences cause new connections and that certain behaviors enhance our ability to increase our capacity for growth. In the end, it has been determined that we have approximately 86 billion neurons in our brains with a firing capacity of up to 1,000 trillion synaptic connections. The more times the synapsis (connections) are fired, the stronger they get.

Furthermore, it has also been established that we have more neurons in our hearts than in our brains. As spiritual beings, we need to retrain ourselves to respond to the electrical impulses from our hearts instead of those in our brains. Our brains are meant to be hard drives that hold memory data, but our hearts are meant to be the transducers of our soul, which houses our higher intellect.

The continual collision amidst the chaos of this multiplex of data is what ultimately leads to decay or demise in the mind and body. We then age and become ill or diseased and repeat the cycle of death and rebirth – having countless chances to refine our approach. It is believed by many that there have been eras in human history where we lived much longer lives because we were more aligned with our spirits and there was also more oxygen on planet Earth.

Because of our state of evolution at this point, we will accelerate our growth while in a single embodiment and will not have to reincarnate so often in order to bring ourselves into alignment. Rather than resolving only a few issues in a lifetime, we will now be able to resolve all of our issues and begin anew within the same lifetime. This has much to do with the mass incarnation of Ascended Masters and spiritual teachers at this time.

There is a formula for rebirth or reinstatement of the authentic self and it takes about three years of complete dedication. Stuart Wilde used to call this the thousand-day climb.

According to Wilde:

"Our life's journey of self-discovery is not a straight line rising from one level of consciousness to another. Instead, it is a series of steep climbs and flat plateaus that take place within our spiritual perception and psychology.

We begin our spiritual understanding in a mundane place: the ordinary world of survival, where the ego reigns supreme, and tribal attitudes and ideologies are promoted as sacrosanct. The plane of day-to-day existence that most experience as "life" - this is what I call "tick-tock".

When an individual is bored with tick-tock and wants more -- when they crave a higher awareness -- then changes at a deep inner level take place. This is especially so if the individual starts to control the ego with discipline.

Looking within, their energy quickens, and they begin the long, slow climb out of the consciousness of tick-tock. Usually the climb from tick-tock up to the first inner plateau of awakening takes about a thousand days.

Soon you realize that in order to sustain your progress upwards, you have to discard much of your mental and emotional weight. When you become less cluttered, new perceptions come to you quick and fast. The inspiration of your rising consciousness infuses you with a new vigor; you want to align to a new energy -- possibly a new career that is more spiritually aligned or has more meaning, except that you don't clearly see what direction to take.

The best thing to do is to concentrate on the climb -- work on yourself rather than trying to carve out a new career just yet. If you head out too early, you'll shoot yourself in the foot. I have seen it happen a thousand times: an individual has become so inspired by their new perspective and their desire to abandon tick-tock that they have set themselves up in a new business -- usually related to self-help, alternative healing, or assisting others in some way -- before they really have the energy, perception, or capital to pull it off. They usually falter or go bust, or they never get off the ground. Their self-confidence level will not yet let them feel secure with their changes, so they cannot pursue the knowledge and experiences necessary to complete the climb.

Instead, do this: Recognize that what you are doing at this moment is changing and climbing -- nothing else. Simplify your life, and support yourself any way you can, providing it does not take too much of your time and energy. Or, you may decide to hold onto your tick-tock job. It's better to do that and have a strong financial backing to your quest than to be terribly spiritual. A third possibility is to keep your former means of financial support in place and begin a new venture, perhaps on a part-time basis.

Once the thousand-day climb is over, you reach the first plane of understanding. As you consolidate on that inner plateau of consciousness, you'll find that opportunities in the external world will begin to emerge. At first, they seem rather small and relatively unimportant. Follow them: they will lead to greater things. It matters not if you head up the wrong path a little way as it will help you learn about yourself and your needs. Eventually, you are bound to find what you seek.

As you make the inner journey from one plateau to the next, the ego's dominance over your life is loosened, and the light of the Infinite Self begins to melt it somewhat. When those melt-downs occur, they seem to your psyche as if bits of your personality are dropping off. In those periods, you will feel overwhelmed by the thought that you are dying, but you are not dying -- your ego is. When the sensation becomes oppressive, put yourself on a vigorous discipline of some kind -- fasting, silence, meditation, whatever. The negative thoughts will pass, and eventually the ego will agree to lessen its grip on your life." (End of Excerpt)

A Course in Miracles refers to the moment an ascent or climb begins as "A little willingness." This infuses the heart chakra with violet energy and then the life of the individual begins to unwind and a new one emerges from the ashes. This is why I chose Violet Phoenix for my publishing company name – my books are about transformation and the phoenix portrays this event accurately.

I point this out to dispel any myth that one may become a master or an intuitive in a weekend seminar. We may gather a great deal of information from a book or a seminar/workshop, but we have to actually do the work and have the experiences. It is much like other professionals who do internships and write lengthy thesis papers. We have to become the real deal in order for us to claim it and all of this takes practice and patience.

Everything we learn, master and become is stored in our chakras, which follow us into each lifetime. Everything we gain is not lost – it goes with us. Think of the chakras as the flash drive. This is how proficient musicians and geniuses blossom when they are toddlers. They are building on mastership from prior lifetimes.

Metaphysics as the study of how the etheric works through the physical, recognizes that everything is programmed to rise, even if it takes a detour or vacation. Higher energies are stronger forces than the lower energies therefore they will pull everything toward them and through the eye of the needle so to speak or into the violet lake of transformation/transmutation. Transmutation is the concept that higher energies dissolve and replace lower energies.

So when we dedicate our being to ascension or rebirth, we initiate a process that will unfold day by day. A Course in Miracles says we can choose the time, but not the curriculum. This is not because something has taken dominion over us, it is that it is much to complicated for our human minds to understand, so we need to trust spirit as we are led through the changes and clearing needed to raise our vibration. The energy will do most of the work for us, but we need to address what we need to address each day and be dedicated to handling things differently than we did in the past.

While the process of clearing marches on, we should feel more refreshed and clear – ultimately healthier because source energy sustains our bodies at every level. We will also become more excited to be alive with higher levels of peace and bliss in tow.

The main point I want to make is this: we simply have to make the decision to become authentic and aligned with spirit. Spirit guides us through the process. Trust the process, do the work that presents itself every day and take time for your self. You should feel a little bit better every day, although there will be rough and challenging days as well. If this seems daunting, think of it this way: You are either dying a little every day or becoming more alive every day. I think the becoming alive more every day is the best choice.

We are mastering a myriad of data connections in the physical as well as the etheric and essentially re-programming the way we feel, think, react....live.

Chapter Three
The Breath of Life

When embarking a spiritual journey, it would be entirely possible to use only the breath to heal and move up the ascension ladder. Naturally, most people will want to use various and multiple modalities, but the great thing about the breath is – it is free and always available to us no matter where we are! It is important to note that in the end, our healing process will not advance and we will not be able to connect to our spirit unless we connect to our breath.

Our breath holds electromagnetic data from the fields that carry data that is so intelligent, precise and miniscule that it would be impossible for our earthly minds to comprehend the divine blueprint it entrains in our being. Breathing is simply something that needs to be revered and respected through faith and results alone.

So, while there are many ways to get in touch with our inner self, we must never lose sight of the fact that the most important aspect is to pay attention to the breath or the center of our being. Because our breath is the physical manifestation of our soul, it is the one aspect of metaphysics that the soul seeker cannot live without.

Even if we have completely lost ourselves, we may begin again by calming our mind and listening to the breath going in and out of our body. This is a guaranteed start over point and we don't need help from someone else to get there. There is also no need to engage in fancy meditations unless one chooses to do so.

The spiritual and physical benefits of learning to work with the breath are life changing primarily because it does a bunch of the work for us and us clears levels that we would not otherwise be able to clear by any physical means.

It may be difficult at first to focus on breathing so I suggest placing reminders in strategic locations until it becomes more automatic. Personally, it has taken me years to learn to consistently focus on my breath.

I am not qualified to give medical advice, but some of the things I mention in this chapter will border on medical advice simply because enhancement of the spiritual translates to reparation of the physical. The healing affects of spiritual work are something that most spiritual teachers and seekers acknowledge, but some medical professionals do not and they can be a bit jumpy.

At the same time, there are indeed many health care professionals and studies that substantiate the healing nature of spiritual practices. A thorough study of information available in medical journals will demonstrate that the information is out there and readily available, yet it is conveniently sequestered, presumably so that the pharmaceutical market may thrive.

The benefits received from connecting with breath are:

Energizing the cells with life giving oxygen

Connecting with our inner space

Connecting with our guidance system

Connecting with the creative portal

Clearing the energy fields

Sending our life force energy into the day

Grounding

Focusing

Brain Food

Activation of the Vagus Nerve

Aside from being the portal to our soul, the most basic and obvious physical benefit of breath work is the energizing of our cells. We have a strong tendency to be in our heads and to breath in a shallow fashion. There have even been times on our planet when there was more oxygen to be had – period.

Each breath delivered more of this life force to our bodies. Let's not forget that we also absorb oxygen through our skin. This may be a reason to believe that we did indeed live longer in some of the earlier human evolutionary cycles.

All spiritual modalities such as yoga, Tai Chi, Qi Gong, etc. engage the breath. The Lamaze childbirth method, developed in the 1940's and used to this day, focuses on breathing. All you need to do is draw in a few gentle breaths and you will see why. With just a few breaths, you will experience a higher level of inner peace and immediately feel the tingling in the cells of your body as you infuse them with life.

I don't believe that it is necessary to sit a certain way or to breath a certain way. It is entirely up to the individual, but if we are going to learn to live our lives connected to our breath, it needs to be a habit that flexible and natural and will serve us in all of our daily activities. Getting accustomed to simply allowing the breath to gently flow in and out of the body is my suggestion.

Breathing enhances our ability to tap into the Law of Attraction. Breath is our way of letting the Universe know where we are. The electromagnetic field of our soul should be fully anchored in our physical bodies because the energy of our soul pulsates magnetic data into the physical realm in order to direct our path, and attract the things we need. When we are not grounded, it is not possible to manifest because our needs cannot find us and magnetically draw to our energy field.

The additional benefit to aligning with the breath is that it is impossible to be centered in the breath without being in the moment and firmly established in the feeling center, which is the creative portal.

What you seek also seeks you.

Breathing places us into the moment and out of our heads. When all other reasoning fails to get us back on track, paying attention to the breath will do it. It is not possible to draw in a relaxing breath without withdrawing from places that are not in our best interest. This action will not only show us those things that have a hold of us, but it will also show us what we are having trouble letting go of. Pay attention to that which keeps you from focusing inward and ask yourself why.

When we gently draw in a breath we refocus our consciousness and realign with the wisdom of our soul. This state will likely result in the gleaning of insight for a given situation, at the same time refreshing our cells and our brain with Source energy, further separating us from the chaos and cacophony. The trick is to stay in this place long enough to begin to feel the connection. Even if we stay in this space for a few moments, the answers will start to come into focus.

Breath displaces other energies and locations, creating a space where the soul becomes the focus of attention and attraction.

We may also use gentle breathing to clear discordant energy out of our aura and our holographic field. Upon gently breathing, we should feel at least a certain level of peace, clarity and strength. If not, that means that discordant energies in our chakra system or other energy fields are blocking this good feeling. We have to regularly practice looking inward and discovering the issues that may be blocking the awareness of our soul. Journaling, watching for repeated patterns and doing general clearing exercises are things to do in order to gain improvements in energy.

This said, one of the reasons we may have a tendency to avoid our breath is because it highlights things we need to deal with. We may errantly believe that disassociation with the things that make us uncomfortable is better than dealing with them. Hopefully when you do your breathing work, you find some good stuff along with some challenging stuff.

I recall the first time I realized I needed to focus on my breath – the area I became aware of upon breathing and focusing inside was about the size of a pea. My inner guidance spoke to me at that moment and said, "Focus on this and you cannot go wrong." Furthermore, it said, "Build this like a muscle." I had already done a great deal of clearing and re-established the connection to my soul, but through the years had internalized a large number of things once again.

I could see as I looked into my energy field that only

a miniscule part of my being was truly aligned with my soul and everything else about me was completely cluttered with other people's agendas and projections. It was time for me to build my center instead of responding to my surroundings.

It takes time to clear the things that don't resonate with our soul, but it begins by clearing one day at a time and one thing at a time. It also takes constant vigilance, as we are still living in a world of discordant, unqualified energies. Ask spirit to help with the clearing and aligning. Our etheric helpers are there for us 24/7. Our etheric help speaks to us through this center as well. Learn to listen to it.

Center in your breath and prime the pump before you begin your day.

It is wise to send your breath out before you so it clears the way as you go through your day to give you a smoother ride and a running start.

Remember that if you send out Love, so too will you encounter Love. If you send out anger and frustration, you will encounter anger and frustration. Naturally, I am speaking of sending out a Loving breath full of Love – pure potential and possibilities for all that you encounter. Breathing into your day is not meant to be a selfish maneuver, it is meant to bring Source energy into the world to benefit all. If you consider yourself to be a light worker, this practice is vital to entraining higher energy on the planet.

Breathing and the Vagus Nerve...

The following description of the Vagus nerve is not meant to be scientific, but instead more of a synapsis. If you are interested in this topic, I suggest you spend some time learning more about it. I am giving a general overview so you may understand the value and importance of breathing and working with the feeling center.

The Vagus nerve originates at the base of our skull in the cerebellum of the brain and runs into the neck and branches into two parts then down and around most of our major organs like the heart, the lungs, the liver, the stomach, the pancreas, the intestines reaching out into virtually every major organ in the abdomen. It controls a vast range of bodily functions including digestion, heart rate, blood pressure, inflammation and immunity as well as sweating and even the gag reflex. (From the website, BodyScience-Massage.com by Stephanie Blaisdell)

When we breath into our entire being instead of being shallow breathers, we enhance the functioning of the Vagus nerve.

Because the portion of the nerve that delivers information from the brain to the body's systems is smaller than the portion that delivers information from the body to the brain, it stands to reason that is critically important to work with the feeling center and the neural connections that have been established in that region over time in order to reestablish a healthier state of being. A healed feeling center will thusly direct the rest of the body and brain.

Our thinking and our feelings are sending information back and forth in all that we do.

In my books I talk about the feeling center or the instinctive center. Some people talk about gut instincts, but I consider those instincts to be more basic and primitive. When I talk about the feeling center, I am talking about all of the neural connections and energetic data in the region between the neck and the hips. We can live without our limbs, but we cannot live without our vital organs or an approved replacement device! Our feeling center directs the communications and ultimately the functionality of our entire being. The signals from this area are sent to the brain and registered there for future use and retrieval.

After millions of signals are sent back and forth through the nervous system, we begin to develop automatic responses based on prior experiences. As we progress in life, building upon past experiences over and over again, life becomes a self-fulfilling prophecy and then it no longer matters whether or not the "thing" in front of you is deemed "good" or "bad", your reaction will be based on prior experiences.

Because the home I grew up in was so hostile and volatile, all uncertain events that I encountered throughout the balance of my life produced a fight or flight response in me. When our bodies and minds go into this mode, adrenalin is released, causing a clinching of the heart muscle with a subsequent cascade of cortisol is pouring into the blood from the liver. The cortisol then signals to the body and the pancreas not to produce insulin. Consequently, after many, many years, the reaction became increasingly worse, with each new experience building on the past. My body would go into fight or flight response if I did so much as drop something on the floor.

This pattern had created a physiology that was completely out of whack and the result was type 2 diabetes or more accurately described, metabolic syndrome. Naturally, the medical establishment immediately wanted to give me pharmaceuticals (with side effects) for the situation, but I had already recognized that my issue was an engrained energetic pattern.

By identifying the issue and slowing down, I recognized that I my body was responding to everyday occurrences as though my life was being threatened. Seeing that my mental body was sending a signal to my physical body when there were happenings, I worked on reprogramming my mental disposition as well as my visceral responses and in time, I stopped reacting this way. It took a couple years. All of this was internalized – I was not acting out. I imagine that an entirely different set of symptoms would have developed if one was the type that acts out in response to situations.

The main point of being in the moment and aligning with our breathing is it allows us to isolate our issues and handle one thing at a time. Otherwise everything continues to be a tangled up mess and it is very difficult to do any healing work or stay in balance at all.

When all else fails, breathe.

Chapter Four
Balancing Karma

We come into each lifetime with karmic agendas. Karmic agendas direct our curriculum for the given lifetime. Our higher self works with the karmic board before we incarnate and we choose our family and various other things in order to propel our lower self (the earthly version of our self) into higher consciousness. Eventually, our lower self should come into alignment with our higher self and become the out-picturing of our soul rather than a chaotic conglomeration of imprinting.

Anything that is not Love is karma.

Because we have been born into a society that values things other than spiritual growth, most of us have missed the proper processing of our karmic lessons or experiences. Many, not all, have been wounded and diminished by challenges instead of using them to propel their growth upward. This has resulted in serious personality distortions across the board. Why do you think it is so inspiring to see the story of a person who took adversity and turned it into something positive? It is inspiring because it sparks our spirit similarly when we witness the truth of our existence in another human being.

Because our body and soul were designed to work in harmony with one another to carry out a unique experience on Earth, anything that is not in resonance with that becomes discordant energy. Continued development of discordant energy wreaks havoc on the spirit and life of an individual as well as those they encounter.

My early exposure to the concept of karma came from a description I received from a Hindu woman at the airport who told me if I gave her a nickel, even though she didn't deserve it, I would create good karma for myself because I had done a good deed. That's kind of like paying it forward, which is effective with regard to the law of attraction; it is not the type of karma I will be talking about here.

A little later on, a close friend of mine told me that karma was payback and it wasn't always obvious what was being balanced because the action may result from a previous lifetime. There are instances where a soul has set up a situation where they have to learn forgiveness and therefore they encounter a horrific or difficult scenario in order to learn the spiritual lesson. This too is an interesting notion, but not the type of karma I will be talking about here.

The type of karma I am going to be discussing is karmic balancing. In a sense, I am introducing a new concept of karma because I have not heard this discussed very much in the spiritual community. I have received information throughout my life from the unmanifested and the realms of the Masters with regard to this topic. The view I have developed is also experiential in nature because it comes from wisdom derived from many years of doing intuitive readings and observing why things happen. This has allowed me to see how energy is directing the things that go on in our lives and in our bodies.

Everything is being reflected or highlighted to show us what we need to balance.

Most of the time, what is happening on an energetic level is not obvious on the level of personality. The reason people have so much trouble working through relationship difficulties is what is being shown on the outside is a distortion of what is happening on the inside. Years upon years of distortion almost bury a problem so deeply that it becomes unrecognizable and unreachable.

If we could begin looking at problems from an entirely different viewpoint, we would begin to see consistency and we would then be able to take responsibility for the issues and fix them. There are different ways to approach this and gain clarity and I will get into that shortly.

To begin with, we can't get clarity on our karmic situations if we are wearing them like a tight garment. We need to gain the ability to neutralize, depersonalize and look at things from a non-judgmental standpoint – or seek a professional who can do this for us!

To help with the unraveling of the lower mind, once again try stepping out of smallness of the human struggle and rise up over the earth to observe its perfection. Look at the deep blue oceans full of life and abundance. Look at the weather systems and atmosphere keeping our planet at a temperature conducive to supporting so many life forms. I am going to suggest this several times in this book.

This amazing perfection and beauty was borne of all of that chaos created by the big blast several billion years earlier. It happened because everything was divinely designed and programmed to be what it is. Therefore, regardless of what we do to steer things off course, the energy will always correct our efforts and its force is much stronger than our will to corrupt it.

We were designed to be whole, perfectly connected beings with full access to all of the intelligence and beauty of the Universe. Science demonstrates that a stomach cell has genetic instructions that cause it to be a stomach, a iron ingot has the atomic structure that causes it to be iron, and water morphs from one substance to another to fulfill its purpose as do all other elements. Our soul also has an intelligent design and metaphysical attributes that cannot be diminished or destroyed. It is best to learn how to cooperate with them.

If you see this period of human difficulty as just a hiccup in the evolution of the solar system, it may be obvious that we too are seeking that which we are designed to become and all that is wrong is that we are not quite whole yet – or we are not aligned with our wholeness. Nobody can really take our power away although they may try and try again.

All of the human drama we are experiencing right now is but a moment in the life of creation. Yet, the suffering for humanity is real. Physical pain and mental turmoil are incredibly uncomfortable. We need to stop getting so hung up on the seriousness of it and restore our fullness so we can get on with things.

Karmic missteps only need to be corrected - not judged, punished or returned. Whereupon we lay judgment, punishment, or retribution, we create more karma. It is time to take a different view of things so we can rise to meet the new energy and enjoy Heaven on Earth.

We shouldn't use relationships as a place to hide from reality. Most relationships are imbalanced –

with the result being love/hate relationships. If we would recognize that the reason for the original attraction was karmic balancing, it would be easy to identify and correct the issues therein. Naturally, there are many other things going on as well and every relationship has its strong points. Ideally, all parties in relationship groupings would take responsibility for their own growth, but we have a strong tendency to blame.

If you want to rise and become self actualized, you will need to take 100% responsibility for your ascent. Even though you deserve "better people" or "better circumstances", you will need to take the things you have in front of you right now and use them to propel you to higher heights. Our relationships show us where we stand if we allow them to be a mirror that reflects our missing pieces. Unless two people are working in perfect harmony and aligned with Source, there is work to be done in order to raise the vibration.

In the past we romanticized the notion of finding the partner of our dreams and we pined for the person who would make us happy and sweep us off our feet, so we would be elevated to a higher level of bliss. True spiritual growth comes from recognizing that all we need is within. I know that tastes like old chewing gum by now, but bear with me. At the most basic level, the Love we need to sustain us is in our own hearts. A heart full of Love makes one feel that there is nothing missing.

I have been through the process and I can vouch for the fact that there is nothing better than reconnecting with your own source of bliss because it is with you wherever you are, 24/7. It no longer matters what others do or say. It is an amazing feeling to always feel at home in your own body.

For instance, if your significant other is emotionally distant and this bothers you, it means you need to develop a closer relationship with your emotions and embrace them without another's acknowledgement. We get what we need to propel us upward. If we were handed this attribute from the outside, we would never develop it on the inside. If our soul has a goal of emotional fulfillment, or our early imprinting created a wounded feeling center, then we will consistently be challenged to work on this issue interiorly. People and events that challenge us or trigger us will continue to show up until we do something about it. Simply affirming that we deserve better will not fill the bill. Healing modalities are many and each person needs to determine what works for them. There is also etheric help available. The first thing we do is identify and own the issue.

Imbalances exist on many levels. We have self karma, group karma and relationship karma. Here is a list of common imbalances:

Yin/yang
Outgoing/Shy
Male/Female
Powerful/Easily Overpowered
Taker/Giver
Growing/Sluggish
Self Starter/Follower

Although we have certain engrained personality traits that are unique to our soul that are meant to be enhancements, we need to examine if we have gone to the negative extreme of a personality trait. This too is an indicator of imbalance. For instance, many people who seek spiritual knowledge are people who are way too giving. It is good to be a giver, but when a giver is consistently encountering takers, it is a sign of an imbalance. On the flipside, a person who has very much and is always sick and tired and has trouble sleeping may do much better if they begin to be more generous with what they have.

There are some instances where imbalances are ok as long as the participants are honest about it. The teacher/student, parent/child, healer/patient are examples. The relationship is karmic if one is lying or taking advantage of the other, engaging in power struggles or manipulating.

After we have checked our imbalances, it is time to look at how the thoughts that we are generating are affecting our physiology. I call this self-karma.

Whenever we feel physical discomfort, it is time to slow down and check the thought system that created it. Often, over-thinking causes headaches. Getting a headache? Neck ache? Check to see if you are toiling over something, grinding teeth, going into mental gyrations. If the headache subsides when you slow down your thinking, that was the problem.

Please note, a headache can be from a physical issue or a side-affect from a medication also.

Self karma is also created when we are carrying disqualified and discordant energy. Energy that is of the lower realms causes us to mis-perceive current circumstances and will cause us to be triggered. In plain language, this is called over-reacting. Examine your triggers and figure out where they came from. They are important teachers. My mother and step-father were heavy drinkers so I always hated the sound of ice-cubes in a glass. It was like someone scratching a chalk board to me. I used to avoid people with icecubes rattling in their glasses, but that was frustrating and futile. When I resolved my issues around my mother and step-father's drinking, the irritation with the sound evaporated.

Even if not evident immediately, all ill-thinking will show up as a physical manifestation eventually. Bio-feedback studies have been done to substantiate this. I always suggest to my readers that they try out a few exercises with regard to changing of the thoughts to note where it is felt in the body. Change a thought and notice the shift in the biology or relative comfort.

Many religions and cultures have tried to determine what maladies are indicated by the part of the body that is diseased or ill. When you read this on websites, etc., take them with a grain of salt. I don't think we have refined this science. We have done very well with acupuncture, herbology, chiropractic, and homeopathy in establishing the inner connections. We have a way to go on connecting our behavior with health issues. As we progress in energy healing modalities, it would be very beneficial.

In my observation, common physical manifestations of issues are:

Knees, feet and ankle problems – Burdens
Back problems – overworking
Neck Problems – Disconnection of Heart and Head
Headaches – Overthinking and worrying
Endocrine, hormonal and digestive issues – long term imbalances
Shoulder Pain – Right Side/Moving Forward in life – Left/Past

Ask your body why it is experiencing pain in a certain region. Get accustomed to listening to it. If something is wrong and it is not obvious, ask you soul to help you find the cause of your difficulty or pain. I you focus on one thing at a time, spirit will surely help you through karmic resolution.

We then move to the issue of energy cords between people in couplings or groups. When we are actualized and in balance, we rely on our inner connection/strength to connect to all we need. In co-dependent relationships, we create energy cords that go both ways. Often we feel and behave in ways that are not in our highest integrity because we are corded with others. We will also feel the pain and imbalances of people we are corded with.

Examples of cords are:

Heart cords – Communication (this is more or less ok) or dependency on someone else's energy

Mental cords – Communication or wanting to know what someone is thinking

Neck cords – very often are from someone wanting to silence another

Sacral chakra cords – usually sexual relationships

Cords are indicators of dependency and power issues and very often hidden agendas. Learn to sense where you have cords and ask the cord what the agenda is. The agenda will be an indicator of the imbalance. For instance, the heart cord where one individual is corded into the other is a situation where one person feels they need to caretake or carry another who feels powerless. This is ok in the mother/infant relationship, but not in mature or spiritually developed relationships. Heart cording can also indicate possessiveness.

Because we pick up other people's feelings from cording, we need to deal with the issue in order to have clear intuition. If not, we will not be clear about what is accurate and where the information is coming from. It is hard to access the intuitive, instinctive, creative center when vibrations from energy connections to others are creating static.

I have found books by Jose Stevens and Rich Ralston to be very helpful with regard to cording and energy interference. These authors and others through time have ascribed certain aspects of life to the different chakras. I too believe that the different chakras represent different areas of our human/spiritual experience. This study can be very useful in determining what karma or discordant energy needs to be purified.

Pain, discomfort or stress in a given area of the body is normally an indicator of issues in that area of development. For instance, solar plexus chakra imbalances will result in digestive and manifestation issues. I have asked my body what the problem is and with practice, it tells me.

Although it is hard to achieve, even people who live in the same home can be energetically autonomous. People who are having sexual relationships *cannot* be energetically autonomous however. Be careful who your sexual partners are if you don't want to take on another person's karma.

In long-term relationships, change can be a very threatening thing because it upsets the status quo and indeed a person who is willing to grow and change is likely to leave a relationship if the other person is not doing the same.

The way to heal karma is to observe closely every day what is not in full integrity in your self, environment and relationships. This is why it is important to slow down and live more deliberately, allowing plenty of time for healing and reflection. Without this, there will be no journey upward.

We only have a very small slice of reality to deal with and our time on Earth is limited. As much as our individual struggle does not do harm to eternity, the need to take care of problems is evident in the discomfort we feel so we don't want to keep lingering in the darkness longer than necessary.

Whereupon our feeling center becomes larger and clearer, we become a greater attractor field for the things we need for life in the physical dimension.

Chapter Five

Soul Mate Relationships

Our relationships will change as we change our relationship with our self. A spiritual quest should entail a journey to the center of our being and a strong connection to our soul. Once a strong connection is made to the foundation of our being and all the triggers are healed and removed, relationships will become natural and easy. I believe that the biggest distraction from the path to spiritual growth is the expectation that our soul mate will arrive along with our dream house and the car we have always wanted. It is not that straight forward and most often not like the fairy tale we hope it would be.

Seek ye first the kingdom of God and these things shall be added unto you. This is perennial wisdom and should not be taken lightly. I know I have mentioned this before, but we must always remember that what we seek outside of us (with the exception of a filet minon done medium well and a glass of merlot) is available on the inside. Somehow, we have lost our focus and tried to find work arounds. Our spirit holds all of the energies that we long for. I promise. Anything that comes from the outside is just the frosting.

In the meantime, all of the relationships, jobs and experiences we have are our teachers. Once we become the embodiment of Love, we can breeze through life on the wings of Angels, but until then it is best not to avoid the challenging things we are presented with. This is how people become lonely – they are avoiding their challenges and hiding away from society because they are too wounded to function.

Relationships will have an even stronger pull when we have things to balance within ourselves. Once we are balanced, we don't feel the need, yet we are capable of having limitless relationships that do not have agendas. This is an interesting paradox, but it is the way things work because of the law of attraction.

I will begin with our strongest soul mate connections. We have twin flames, which are the other half of our self. While our soul does not have a gender, in order to incarnate on the physical plane, a soul has to be either male or female. This leaves an energetic portion of their being either in the etheric or in another body. This metaphysical disposition is a strong driver in our quest for a soul mate. We have a strong tendency to feel that something is missing because in a way it is. However, focusing inward aligns us with the energy of our full being including that which is not incarnated or otherwise disposed.

It does not matter what our sexual orientation or anatomical gender is in this lifetime. The balancing act is the same for all forms of existence.

Next, we have twin souls, which are souls that were born into the cosmos at the same time we were. Often these people have parallel paths – the same or very similar life experiences and challenges. I have met at least one of mine and the similarities in our lives are astonishing – much as the similarities that have been noted in the lives of fraternal twins who were separated at birth. These individuals may or may not be the same sex or sexual orientation as our selves.

There are also soul agreements that occur before incarnation and also while we are walking the Earth. We have soul relationships in other dimensions and we made agreements to meet on the physical plane some where along the way. I am sure you know who those people are – the ones where you have instant recognition or an instant feeling of comfort or warmth. They often meet and become the Beatles and such.

I have done many readings for people who have met one of these soul mates where the other one is still asleep or loaded with triggers and fears and consequently unable or unwilling to recognize the one who is more awake and now seeking professional help. It is frustrating for the ones who are more aware and more willing to take chances. Often they must give up on the relationship for their own mental and emotional well-being if the other does not want to participate. This can be a mind-bender.

Complications can and do arise in soul mate relationships. Often times, soul mates of ours are unavailable because of other commitments or substance abuse issues. It is possible to meet a person who was a spouse of ours in a past life, while in this lifetime, they have a different sexual orientation or are incarnated as a familial role that would make a romantic relationship inappropriate this time around. People usually think of the twin flame as a romantic partner, but what if that is rendered impossible due to circumstances? If this was the case, would you not have to learn how to love them unconditionally if you could not have them, be with them nor influence them in any way even though they were the other half of you? Imagine how this would affect a person energetically if they held any ill feelings toward the other half of their self? The karmic impact in soul mate relationships is much more powerful than it is in general because of the immediacy created by the energetic relationship.

Finally, there are also people who are from our soul group on the other side. Then there are groups within groups. For instance, I am in the soul group Archangel Michael, but more specifically Melchezedek.

Rather than leaving behind a trail of tears, it is a good idea to arrive at a peaceful conclusion for all of the important relationships you have had. Your spiritual quest will benefit tremendously from this practice. We have difficult soul mate relationships and absolutely magical ones. Make sense of everything that happened, derive some benefit from the experience and let go with unconditional love. If there is a perfect soul mate for us, they will only appear after we have become entirely aligned with our self and learned how to love and appreciate all of those who have gone before.

Chapter Six
Accessing Your Internal GPS

Development of intuition is critical because we need to learn to define and discern energies and energy signatures in order to navigate the path of our soul and keep our energy in integrity. It also makes our lives much, much easier to live and more fruitful.

When it comes to the subtle energies, we encounter them whether we want to or not, so it is a good idea to practice working with them in order to gain discernment and clarity.

Not only do we have messages flowing through our physical body and etheric energy, we have data drifting around in our holographic field. We also have energy cords and connections to other people. Ideally, we want to keep our energy free and clear of all outside connections and past programming.

The holographic field stores data from our experiences as well as mental imaging from others and our selves. Our chakras also hold information that is part of our past life history as well as our current incarnation. We store the images of our childhood and past relationships and this is part of the reason that we still feel influenced by the past even though we work hard to heal and restructure it.

We need to learn how to clear our fields so that the information there does not interfere with current guidance coming from the unified field. While these fields are not usually visible to the human eye, this information does attract and create through law of attraction to a certain extent and does give off signals and interference because it has energy. This is why we often wonder why things seem to be manifesting in a chaotic manner even though we believe we have clear intentions. When we heal, we must heal on many different levels or things will continually re-appear. Sunlight, color work and salt baths help clear the outer aura.

We often are not aware of where our thoughts and feelings are coming from. When we embark on the journey of self-discovery, it is important to understand all of the energies that play/ed a part in defining who we are. Once we determine the ingredients that have become our reality, we can make changes if we so desire. What was right for someone else may not be right for us.

We can use imagery and breathing as well as various other energy healing modalities to keep our fields clear. Being in the sun at midday and immersing our bodies in salt water, especially the natural ocean, does a great job of clearing our etheric web and other energies. If natural modalities are not readily available, we can practice imagery, invoking colors and using our breath to clear. We can read books about energy healing or seek the help of others.

Ideally, we should know and Love our soul; we should feel like we are anchored in Source energy and that it is guiding us. We should be in touch with all of its higher attributes and feel comfortable in our skin. We should feel warm, brilliant and safe. We should be able to sit in its warmth and softness, and witness the outside world without being harmed or jarred by it. When completely mastered, this disposition gives one a full clear view of things. The greatest intuition and creativity comes from this space. Intuition increases with every bit of clearing and healing we perform.

Clearing is a long process, so expecting to take off full throttle will only slow the progress, as we must let the wisdom of Source energy help us to dismantle the discordant elements of our programming, step by step, day by day. What we do have control over is making sure that we align with our center and validate it, no matter how small it may initially seem.

When we nurture our inner light, breathe life into it and then send it outward, becomes louder and stronger. Inner guidance is like a muscle. In time, we become acutely aware of its energy signature or feeling. Ignoring our soul and internalizing the outside world is how we became dysfunctional to begin with, so it is time to change our habits. It is wise to be patient with the process and enjoy the increased benefits along the way.

As we build our connection to our soul, it grows much, just as a well attended garden does.

As we learn to identify and prioritize, we need to get familiar with the fields of data that we must contend with at all times. For the most part, we receive subtle data from:

Our mind (decisions and observations)

Our instinctive center (advancing or withholding)

The people around us (cacophony)

Our soul group (impulses, creativity and cacophony)

People we are corded to (energy, impulses and cacophony)

Electrical fields and radio signals (mental and physical interference)

Our inner guidance (visionary, audible or symbolic)

Our guides (visionary, audible or symbolic)

The Astral Planes (out of the blue, taunting, interfering, dangerous)

Countless other sources

Discernment:

All of these sources of data have a frequency or vibration. Each particle and type of data also has an energy signature. An energy signature is much like a personality in that it has a conglomeration of characteristics that make it unique. For instance, the angelic realms feel soft and uplifting and the messages are empowering, clear and supportive regardless of the content. The astral planes feel heavy, often inducing a headache and messages from this realm are often scary, pushy, misleading or manipulative. The astral plane energies are also pesky and intrusive.

Very often, intuitive mediums want to hold something from the person that they are inquiring about. The energy signature is what they are tuning into and it helps them differentiate between the energies surrounding their clients.

It takes conscious, deliberate practice and slowing down to learn the discernment necessary to recognize the energy signature of the different fields and to learn where information is coming from. While I found it easy to sit down and perform a clear reading for a client, I had to practice the discernment needed to navigate everyday things in everyday life because the data in the kinetic planes is inherently confusing and overwhelming and increasing every day.

When we sense someone before we run into them or receive a phone call from them, this is the recognition of the energy signature. In time, we can learn how to recognize many energy signatures.

For instance, when I found myself thinking an un-comfortable thought, I would ask myself, "Where did that come from?" If I was attempting to get things done or run errands and began experiencing mental fog and indecision, I knew that I had picked up on the massive communication jam that is the mental planes. As a matter of fact, most of what crosses our mental body is coming from the collective. Don't believe everything you think!

When we learn to channel information from our feeling center to our brain, instead of picking up debris from the mental planes, we then begin to live a life that is directed by our spirit.

When I experience uncomfortable or confusing thinking and directions, I stop and re-center, allow-ing myself to begin again. With practice and delib-erate intention, remaining centered becomes second nature. There is always a positive solution to every problem, but we have to seek it in the mix of data we will inevitably encounter. I don't like to block out undesired data. I like to create filters. Let's say that I have neighbors who are always arguing I can feel the tension and hear the noise. The filters I would use are: 1) They are on their own path and handling things to the best of their ability and 2) I don't believe in conflict. If I get annoyed, judgmental or freaked out about the bickering, its energy will come into my energy field.

We are only bothered by energy if we are enmesh-ing with it somehow, either by over focusing, judging or mirroring our own deficiencies. Try it out and see how it works for you. I have learned to let my soul guide me to take issue with the things I should take issue with. Sometimes we are supposed to get involved in something. We first examine the ego because the ego takes issue with almost everything.

When we position our mental focus on the future or the past, or into someone else's energy, we get the clutter and all the bad news that goes along with it. Although it has long been a normal human practice to allow our consciousness to travel all over the place, it is actually one of the behaviors that keeps us ungrounded, which is of no benefit to anybody whatsoever.

Grounding is the practice of learning to be in our center or vortex and not in the future or yesterday nor in someone else's head. Doing so will yield better decision-making and give us clearer insights and answers. There will be less conflict for those who move into this higher state of being. Being connected is also the place of creativity where great art, music and writing abilities flourish.

Intuitive guidance is the missing link with regard to many of our problems both personally and collectively.

As we practice working with intuition and inner guidance, we will make mistakes and that is ok. The only way to learn how to use our instincts is trial and error. If we need help, we should consult an experienced intuitive. Even experienced intuitives are always learning. As we learn to normalize intuitive living, we must be compassionate and patient with others and ourselves.

Even though it is very common for a professional intuitive reader to make a mistake by infusing his or her own judgment or to misinterpret something, there is still value in getting a reading. There will always be bits of information that are valuable even if there are parts that are not completely in focus. Let's not throw out the baby with the bath water.

For this reason, it is best to do most of our own work first; this will make it harder to get thrown off by another's input. An intuitive counselor should help us when we are at a fork in the road. We all need confirmation until we get really strong at understanding our inner guidance.

The abilities of intuitive mediums vary tremendously, but this does not mitigate their importance.

We are all in this together and we are learning together as we go. Because intuition has become a necessary life tool, we must get through the awkward stage. I am saying this because I don't want people to get turn off by the industry because a reader was a bit off on their ability to accurately read something. If the truth were known, we sometimes believe a reader to be wrong when it is we who are in denial. Also, a client can block a reader's ability to see clearly if they have too much resistance.

The best readings happen when the querent is prepared and weighed out and stretched their own senses first. This is primarily how we learn to work with energy. We have a circumstance or situation; we ponder the possibilities, and then try to discover the clearest, most resonant answer. We release the outcome to the wisdom of the Universe and then watch things progress.

If things are moving too slowly or nothing is happening in the possible streams, there may be blockages or other avenues and the intuitive medium serves as a sounding board to refine the work that the client has already done.

When we learn to be in the moment and achieve peace and stillness of the mind, we will hear the still small voice and feel the little tugs of our soul. As we master these subtleties, we refine our ability to make strong decisions for our soul journey. This does not happen over night. This is one reason it is considered a part of self-mastership. I full-heartedly encourage people not to give up on their intuition. The darkness hopes that we stay disconnected so it can take advantage of us.

In the end, we are walking away from a paradigm where others have been running our lives because we did not feel we had much choice in the matter. In order to move into an era of greater freedom, we have to come from a place of greater responsibility and that includes trusting our instincts and inspiration.

Clarity...

Discernment is part of clarity, but in order to have mental clarity and subsequent spiritual clarity, we have to be heart centered and have a clear head. Clarity refers more to our clarity of vision and reception than to recognition of energy signatures. Our inner discipline keeps our consciousness in the moment and in our own space while our breath takes us to our center.

Our head is supposed to be the receiver of information from our soul. If we are toiling in our head, we will block the awareness of signals and other information from our soul. Toiling in the head causes brain fog.

Another very important physical sign of being trapped in circular reasoning inside the 'head' is clenching of the jaws or teeth. When our molars touch in the back, they trigger brain activity, which is distracting us from our instinctive center. The harder we are biting down, the more intensely we are holding on to limited thought patterns.

This is one reason people have trouble sleeping. The brain will not stop processing if the molars are touching. The jaw must become loose. We need to learn to feel like a vessel and bathe in the energy of our soul in order to rest properly and rejuvenate on all levels. An active mind keeps all of our systems engaged and eventually they become exhausted and lead to confusion.

Why do people in the new age keep telling us to get out of our head?

The mentally focused mind does not have perception; it only has the ability to access information that it has collected in the past; therefore it ignores a large part of the information needed to provide answers for the now and beyond. It is only when we become adept at sensing and responding to the instinctive center that we become claircognizant and co-creative.

Aligning with the heart connection feels different than the mental and when one is not accustomed to it, it can seem like a dream. Ideas and visions instantly appear in our mind's eye. The heart/soul projects on the mind's eye or screen and provides us with "ah-ha moments" and larger blocks of information that some may call a "knowing" or a *download.*

When we fill up our vessel and make inner focus our point of priority, it can feel a bit like we are on drugs or have been drinking because there is a loosening of the rigid constructs of the brain and logic – the same affect we seek when we use mind altering substances. In time, the brain and physical senses come into alignment and things no longer seem to be out of focus or dream like. In time we learn that the state of mental emptiness is the critical first step in attaining clarity.

Clarity allows for a directed, powerful sense of knowing

The brain should not feel heavy and tired; it should feel light and airy. Initially, upon release of the higher brain cycles, it will feel spongy and confused because it actually begins to reorganize the files to be used more effectively and efficiently by the soul. This is attributed to the fatigue, malnourishment and confusion that are created by consistently maintaining high brain cycle activity. The brain, just like anything else, needs rest and nourishment.

Once we detach and distance ourselves from the brain, it will begin the cleaning process. Science has established that the brain actually washes out the debris that is created by activity on a regular basis only when it is at rest.

On the topic of brain nourishment - high carb diets, energy drinks, alcohol and marijuana as well as a host of pharmaceuticals, rob the brain of healthy nourishment and processing. Alcohol and marijuana in particular, dehydrate the brain cells and water is critical for electrical synapses. Hydration and nutrition are critical components of cell regeneration as well. Healthy fats are also critical to efficient brain function.

Expect to wake up each day with more clarity.

We simply receive added benefit and maintain higher levels of clarity if we give our brains time to rest during the day as well.

Take care not to get trapped in the kinetic fields. As a group, we are connected in the mental planes, just as we are connected in the realm of the heart or spirit. The realm of the heart is the unified field where singularity of purpose and co-creative activity are born. When we go into a space of mental activity, one reason we often get bogged down and mentally fatigued is that our mind is actually joining with the postulations and mental clutter of others in addition to the misfiled information that we hold in our own brains. Then we incur the battle of the minds.

The mental plane is similar to the Internet in that there is an overabundance of information and confusion is inevitable without our center to guide us. What happens is that the ego mind runs through loops of postulations and arguments, exhausting itself in the process. Once again, the reason that this happens is that the information stored there is from the past and is generally not completely adequate for solving whatever situation we currently find ourselves in.

The brain cycle designations that we are familiar with are beta (14 to 30 cycles per second), alpha (eight to 13 cycles per second), theta (four to five cycles per second), and delta (less than 4 cycles per second). Healthy brain cycle activity for an intuitively integrated life style is theta. This may also be referred to as a hypnogogic state.

The term hypnogogic may sound like a person in this state is loopy and disconnected, when in fact the state is entirely contrary to this notion. This state provides us with the perfect balance between the physical and the etheric, allowing us to clearly observe and blend the two. In this state we can carry out great functions. When we encounter someone who is very present, very wise and appearing to be of great authority, you can bet they are in a state of low brain cycle activity and connected to their source energy.

This same concept is the explanation for savants. The excess brain activity that most of us normally have to deal with does not get in the way of the line feed from spirit where true intelligence and creativity is. If there is nothing else that will convince us of the natural genius of the soul, the existence of savants should do it.

When we remain connected to Source, our inner guidance lets us know <u>what</u> we need to know <u>when</u> we need to know it.

Oh, the tangled web we weave…

Although we may do the work that is needed to remain within the frequency of Love, we may be thwarted by information or feelings we receive through cords or entanglements. Familial groupings and life partner pairings are relationships that are more subject to entanglement or enmeshment than others. This occurs when mental, physical and emotional dynamics are interdependent, causing energetic connections between the individuals that often cause the pairings or groups to have trouble defining their own space.

Energetic entanglement also contributes to the difficulty one has when a relationship is ended as the result of separation or death. After being energetically dependent on each other for a long period of time, we lose the ability to know where one ends and the other begins. When there is a separation, there can be a sudden feeling of emptiness, almost like having a phantom pain or limb. Reality often takes a length of time to re-establish itself in our minds and in our energy.

As a result, enmeshment is also one of the primary causes of power struggles in close relationships. While couples cherish their unity, a part of everybody will always fight to be autonomous. The conflict then tends to be blamed on the other person. To the end of having clarity, I believe it is important to understand this dynamic because it is a great energy drain and distractor from clarity.

Not only does enmeshment cause us to confuse our thinking and feelings for another's, we also pick up on another's feelings as a result of empathy. This occurs when we feel someone else's pain because we are energetically standing in their shoes or actually activating cell memory. This is why many couples begin to look like each other and develop similar handwriting after being together for decades.

Furthermore, we can actually get inside someone's head, or conversely, they can be in ours – neither of which is desirable when we are trying to be clear. I like to refer to all of this as psychic politics. I know so many people who are so engaged in psychic politics that they are unable to focus on their own lives.

I know that all of this sounds a bit fussy, but when we desire to become acutely familiar with the energy signature and the intuitive guidance of our own soul, entanglements and enmeshments are the greatest distractions we face in aligning with our soul purpose and higher energies. We were not meant to get our energy from others. We are supposed to get it from Source/God.

When we are not able to relax and enjoy the beauty of the moment and the warmth of inner self, or we feel utterly confused, it means we have interference. When we continually make bad decisions and incur accidents, we have interference. Interference is any energetic intrusion that we allow into our vortex. Each person has different sources of interference and different skills for removing interference. While one individual may have trouble getting out of their head, another individual may not be able to cease churning over relationship issues with another person.

We have to continually get to know ourselves and our beliefs on a deep level, otherwise we will get confused by the information that is flying through the ethers in every situation we encounter. Every moment that we engage in drama is a moment we could be getting to know ourselves and get on with co-creating instead.

Vibrational Attunement and Alignment...

Finally, really clear intuition only flows on a certain frequency and the energetic disposition of the person places them either inside or outside of this frequency. As always, this frequency is Love. The depth to which we reside in this realm determines the breadth of our vision. Translation: The bigger the heart, the greater the connection!

These are the twelve facets of Love. If you want to know more about this subject, please refer to Chapter 4 in this book or a booklet I have written which is called Christ Consciousness Through the Twelve Aspects of Spiritual Love.

Tolerance

Trust

Faithfulness

Honesty

Gentleness

Patience

Joy

Thankfulness

Expansion

Defenselessness

Generosity

Open-Mindedness

The more we are tuned into the frequency of Love, the better our connection and reception to spiritual guidance and the unified field. It is impossible to connect to guidance from a low vibrating disposition.

All the right ingredients...

Breathing, clarity, vibrational alignment, mental stillness and discernment are all characteristics required in order to gain spiritual integrity. Spiritual integrity is the greatest contributing factor to clear and valuable intuition. This may sound really complicated and cumbersome, but think about how long it took to learn to do things the other way

Our personal energy is a part of other energy systems that are all overlapping, interdependent and intermingled, yet we are capable of taking personal responsibility for our own energetic space. When we make the decision to align, everything begins to fall into place. Once we begin to work with the subtle energies, we discover that they are not subtle and in effect – they are actually the only sustainable, reliable power that is available to us and they will grow – eventually outshining other possibilities.

One day soon, living instinctively will be a very

much validated and legitimate way to live. Also, I see a time when the subtle fields are recognized as useful tools and information by the scientific community. Then, we will be able to develop electronic equipment to do much of what intuitives are doing now, disposing of medical misdiagnoses, saving us countless millions on medical and psychiatric care as well!

At the same time, while I believe we will someday develop machinery that will enhance our ability to diagnose more accurately and without damaging invasiveness, I further believe that we will come to understand that in the truest sense, machines will never have the capacity to discern information as accurately or as in depth as a master intuitive because the layers that we have access to are infinite.

Messages from the higher self...

I don't want to burst your bubble, but I am going to get realistic about channeling and conversations with God or other masters. The good news is I will help you replace this notion with something that is even better.

First of all, if God is creation, God does not speak. If God could speak, God would certainly not speak our language. Our language, no matter what the culture of origin is too narrowly focused to handle all that God would tell us if God could. A close comparison would be: if you need to heat your home, you use a heater that you bought at the store that is designed and approved for use on this planet. You would not lasso the sun and put it in your living room. Not only are you not able to do so, success would prove to be disastrous.

Everything is merely an extension of God. We are extensions of God and yes, we have benevolent beings at our beck and call. We need them especially now and they do communicate with us. Communication differs depending on who you are. The way communication between dimensions works is similar to voice translation software in that one dimension communicates with another dimension through vibrations that are translated to fit the dimension and personality type by an intelligent design. It takes time to learn your particular way of communicating with things greater than yourself.

The dimensions are like the colors in the rainbow. Our earthly self accesses our higher self and then our higher self accesses even higher realms and beings.

For instance, an archangel's energy is in a higher dimension, but is omnipresent just as God is. This means their energy is a part of everything that is. Tuning into an Archangel's energy requires the ability to tune into that frequency and the communication will come to the individual in a way that the individual is able to receive it. If someone such as

Doreen Virtue (well known for her communication with Archangels) is seeing or sensing a physically formed being as a particular Archangel, then that is how she needs to or wants to see it.

I communicate with these realms by sensing the frequency. I do not hear a voice or see a singular being. I hear words in the form of vibrations that are immediately translated into my language and imprinted on my mind (temporary drive) where I pick it up. I also get what I call downloads but did not have this ability until I had advanced in my ability to receive information from the unified field. I receive whole packages of information that are deposited in my feeling center or in my mind's eye and data banks.

When you first begin to communicate with your higher self, you will be challenged to access it to find things you have lost or to find your way to a destination when you have lost your way. Your higher self is not going to lead you into difficult territory without teaching you the basics first. Many people have reported to me that they used these common opportunities as a way to develop the connection.

Try asking a question before you go to bed and see if you get answers in your dreams or in the morning when you awake. Take time throughout the day to connect to your soul. Still your mind and listen to your breath going in and out. Pull yourself away from all of the other voices and chaos and see what you sense. Know what your level of ability is.

A well developed feeling center is necessary in order to be a good receptor for spirit. Are you stuck in your head? Is your heart and feeling center closed down or carrying baggage? If so, you've essentially unplugged the receiver.

Now, we have the creative center. The creative center needs to be developed, accessed and clear in order to bring goodies from our soul. Our souls have experience from past lives as well as access to the unmanifested realms of creation. We can pull in those things we are ready for through the same portals we receive intuitive guidance and wisdom.

If you have a particularly busy life with lots of people in it, I suggest taking classes in the things you feel drawn to because doing so chisels out that precious space and time for you to focus only on those things.

Highly developed intuition and creative gifts are usually not born overnight. We need to tend to our garden and spend time there in order for it to grow.

Intuitive Exercises

We may use our inner guidance for anything and everything. As a matter of fact, we can train our minds to run through the systems of our body or the mechanics of an automobile to locate difficulties. Intuition may be used to navigate the best route to the office or to decide which foods to eat in order to maintain a proper balance of nutrients. When we get clear enough, we can receive valuable information from spirit on how to best handle our relationships. The bottom line is that intuition makes our lives much easier. We can use even the most basic activities in life to develop our intuitive guidance system.

Below are some common daily things whose experimentation with is relatively harmless and are common situations that can be used to learn how to side-step judgment and receive clear guidance. Not only do they provide good practice, they help us become familiar with our own unique methods of working with our internal GPS.

Finding a lost object...

One of the easiest lessons in receiving intuitive guidance is to apply it to locating something that has been lost. You know the dance: you have been around the house and through every drawer eight times and you are getting dizzy in the process. What you need to do is completely forget about the lost object. Then, a variety of things may occur. Either you will be doing something entirely different when all of the sudden, out of the blue, you remember where the lost object is. This is your soul's way of letting you know where it is, but we have to get our mind out of the equation in order to get the clarity.

For those who are more instinctive than clairaudient, follow your instincts and impulses in regard to your activities for the day. And you will find yourself engaged an activity that, once you have forgotten about the lost object, leads you to it.

Because people access intuition differently, some may find that they can hone in on the item and follow an energy stream to the object – much like dousing. This method would work well for those who are more clairsentient. I think that this method of location requires a level of skill that most do not possess, but if it works for you, that is wonderful.

Navigating chaos...

The next time you are headed somewhere and you are late, try relaxing instead of tensing up, and then sense your inner guidance leading you through the best route. It is important to follow your instincts because they know the traffic flow and will choose the peaceful, clear route. The law of attraction dictates that if we are tense, we will find ourselves in traffic with other tensed up people.

Stay calm and let the energy lead you and get you to your destination on time. Should you find yourself in a traffic snarl anyway, stay calm and your energy will likely be transferred to others, creating a winning situation for all. I use this calming energy in all potentially volatile situations and it works wonders 99.9% of the time. I have even found that by remaining calm and positive, that the circumstances of the situation will resolve themselves in a positive manner.

In this type of exercise, you are actually learning how to send a given energy out and then learning how to follow it, one moment at a time.

In a jam...

When it comes to making an important decision, we have to stop the postulations and assumptions that our brain makes. We often bounce from one thing to another, going in circles in our mind instead of stepping out of the situation and looking at it from an intuitive vantage point. As always, receiving an answer for a decision may involve either hearing our inner voice or sensing our instincts, or both.

Once I could not find my teenage daughter late at night in an area where she was supposed to be I followed an urge I had to return home even though I hadn't yet found her. While driving and upon calming my mind, I heard the words, she is at home sleeping. The words were very clear. Indeed, when I got home, she was there, sleeping. My urge to go home was correct and the words confirmed it. Someone had driven her home and did not let me know.

Clear intuition requires absolute neutrality – release all attachment to results.

Avoid Empathy...be compassionate instead...

Using focused conscious awareness to read a person or situation is a method of intuiting that I do not recommend. If we put our consciousness in a situation or on a person for longer than a couple seconds, we take on the energy and we pick up another's pain and confusion. As I always say, it is best to receive guidance from our own soul.

Practice present moment awareness...

Probably the most beneficial discipline for developing intuition is practicing present moment awareness. It requires that we have our breath calmly centered in our body, mental activity slowed to the minimum, focused entirely on where we are at the moment with what is in front of us. We can tell if we are doing a good job because we can hear everything that is going on around us and we can feel every inch of our physical body, yet we are focused on our center, allowing it to direct us.

While this is easy to do at certain junctures, it is much harder to apply to all aspects of life including bill paying, grocery shopping, conversations, cleaning, work, etc. It takes time, but with practice, one can live their life from this space.

It has taken me years to learn how to do this most of the time. It comes to the point where the discomfort involved in being off center becomes very obvious. At this point, I find it impossible to live any other way.

Chapter Seven
All Together Now: Aligning the Bodies

In order to experience higher consciousness and heaven on earth, our four main bodies need to be working in harmony. We have the spiritual, physical, mental and emotional bodies that are designed to work together to allow us to be co-creative vehicles on the Earth plane.

Spiritual-Physical-Mental-Emotional

Each of our lives began with adult caregivers who were carrying their own discordant energies and then we spent several years in the learning institutions, which for the most part were designed to groom factory workers. We were trained to conform, to follow directions and submit to authority. The souls that are incarnating on Earth now and in the last few decades are coming in with the goal of becoming entrepreneurs and creative individuals. In order to do so, one needs to be connected to their inner authority rather than the outer. As a result, children have been labeled with disorders such as attention deficit hyper-active disorder (ADHD), attention deficit disorder (ADD) and so on.

If only educators and the educational system would recognize that these children are not defective or naughty! The system is at fault because they are trying to fit square pegs into round holes. We should be learning how to balance and care for all of our bodies from the time we begin life and continue in the school system in the same way we learn academics.

Unfortunately, we are not taught how to actualize our soul journey, so by the time we graduate from the system, we are utterly lost and confused. We go out in the world and bump up against everybody else's confusion and that is why we are sick, addicted, frustrated and tired.

Not much has changed for a couple centuries with regard to schooling people for life. Hopefully people will answer their spiritual calling with regard to educating today's young people so they are fit to handle life to the fullest when they set out to be responsible adults. I think the millenials who were born with a generous portion of cosmic energy, have been hampered by the system in so many ways that many find themselves victims of the chaos, which is entirely un-navigatiable without the proper tools.

So, here we are a society full of people who are going in so many directions that we have a strong tendency to dig out with prescription and recreational drugs or conversely act out toward others. The spiritual movement teaches us that we are these amazing creatures. As an intuitive I can vouch for that. I see all the levels within people. The brilliance is there, yet it is often inaccessible simply because the bodies are not aligned and working together.

While we have a certain amount of leeway as organic beings, there is only so much wiggle room before things go off balance. Each person has their unique strengths and weaknesses in all of their bodies. This is the main reason it is not wise to judge others. You've heard folks say, "Everybody is dealing with something you are not aware of." This is so very true.

When we embark a spiritual journey it is important to understand that it will push the other bodies to come into balance. If the balancing of all the bodies is ignored, inertia will set in and flow will be negatively impacted.

What follows is a description of the healthy states of each of the bodies:

Mental:

The mind and the brain comprise the mental aspect. The mind is the vertex between the physical and the spiritual, while the brain is clearly part of the physical. The mental should not run the show and it should be groomed to serve the spiritual aspect. A spiritual journey begins with energetic willingness and the surrender of the mental to the spiritual.

The brain needs rest and proper nutrition. Pharmaceuticals, recreational drugs, alcohol, overuse and misuse hamper the brain's ability to sort and organize information and build new neurons and connections.

The mind should be clear, calm, organized and seated in the individual's energy (not drifting around in the ethers) and in the moment.

Physical:

The physical body and brain function on the concept of use it or lose it. Furthermore, areas that are in decay may be resurrected by correcting the use thereof. For instance, the bones get stronger with the introduction of weight bearing exercise. The body also needs to be taken care of with regard to nutrition, rest and respect of its biological needs and function. It should feel light, fluid and flexible.

The aura and the holographic fields are also part of the physical and have much to do with how things manifest in the physical world. Thought forms we create as well as those we have experienced and taken on from our environment will be in our holographic field. The aura has all of the vibrations (which can be seen as colors which also have unique vibrations) of our fields.

Often these fields are seen as etheric, but this is not entirely accurate because they only exist in the physical life of the individual. Once the individual transitions, these fields are no longer necessary.

Spiritual:

The soul runs the show and the body and mind need to be receptors of spirit. When they are healthy, they are able to be spontaneous and responsive to the guidance and wisdom of the soul, which moves at the speed of creation. We get locked up when the mind and body lag behind. Conversely, we get jammed up when the mind and the body try to run the show and move faster than spirit or move in their own direction completely. Consistently wanting to get ahead of the game or resisting the prompting of spirit will also have negative physical consequences because we choke off life affirming energy when we impinge the flow of spirit.

Emotional:

The emotional body is the energy portal of the soul. I often refer to it as the feeling center or instinctive center. This is where we store our capacity to love and also improve our connection to our soul. If it is clogged up with pain and anger, it will distort impulses from the soul and or not be recognizable at all. Very often these impulses become warped and cause people to lash out at others. It is important to clear pain from the past and work on self love in order to have a large, healthy feeling center - your dream catcher.

Chapter Eight
Livelihoods vs. Jobs

Whether or not the system or we are ready for it, change is afoot. Notwithstanding the mass spiritual awakening that is occurring, there are many karmic reasons why the way we earn money and the way we serve needs to change.

The lopsided economy is very karmic. For the most part, the economic disparity we see at this point results from the fact that those who are more daring (some good people and some bad people) are getting further ahead than people who are suffering because they are handing their lives over to the daring instead of becoming empowered in their own realm. This situation doesn't have as much to do with the successful people's greed as it does with the sheeple being scared to take chances. To some this will sound harsh but in fact it is empowering. It means we don't have to wait for someone else to change in order for each individual to live a better life.

I am going to quote someone who I have met several times. His name is Joe Sugarman. He is one of the initial founders of Sharper Image and Blublocker sunglasses. He has written several books and textbooks about success. He admits to failure and I'm not sure too many people are willing to be as raw as he when describing his ascent. Here are some Sugarman quotes to get us started on this conversation:

"It's not whether you win or lose in life that's important but whether you play the game. Lose enough and eventually you will win. It's only a matter of time."

"Not many people are willing to give failure a second opportunity. They fail once and it is all over. The bitter pill of failure is often more than most people can handle. If you are willing to accept failure and learn from it, if you are willing to consider failure as a blessing in disguise and bounce back, you have got the essential of harnessing one of the most powerful success forces."

"Each problem has hidden in it an opportunity so powerful that it literally dwarfs the problem. The greatest success stories were created by people who recognized a problem & turned it into an opportunity."

Bashing wealthy and successful people is really popular right now. Yes, many aspects of society have made it very challenging for those on the lower rungs to rise up. Maybe we need to work on some of the society issues. On a personal level, this may be a waste of energy unless it is in your cards to be a social activist. In fact, there will always be several ingredients needed to be successful and without risk and persistence, all the lube in the world won't be enough grease to get the gears to move. Additionally, wealth and success are not always synonymous. Sometimes one comes before the other or without the other.

Most wealthy and successful people have lost a lot of money and friends along the way. I am not condoning walking over people or lying or cheating to get to the top. I am saying that there will be mistakes and there will be changes that need to be made in order to get where we need to be energetically. As I have mentioned, when we change it can be scary to our friends and family. We may either reach for safety or reach for the gold in life. We can't live if we are afraid to die. That's just the way it is.

I realize that in many cases people believe that they have no choice but to stay in an energetic dead end, but we must understand that if we devote over 40 hours a week or more of our energy to someone else's cause, we will not have enough left over to nurture our own dreams. Then we become beholden to them and the rest of the package that comes along with it.

I call this package the machine. Because most of us

are so drained, with or without cash resources, it creates a situation where we have to seek fulfillment on the outside and we pay dearly for it. There is no energy left to take issue with companies that over charge us for services or just plain rip us off. How much of your hard-earned money has been wasted because you did not have time to return something that was faulty? How much are you over-paying for your car that depreciates faster than you can pay it off? Having trouble keeping your credit score high enough to be a player in this game?

It gets to the point where staying down is more painful than the challenges of rising.

The neglecting of our souls and the persistent avoidance of the prompting of our hearts causes us to be enamored with pop culture icons – football players, rock stars, super models, etc. because they give us a temporary charge. Let's start talking about starring in our own lives. Think about how great it would be to jump out of bed in the morning because you can't wait to get to your creative projects and adventures. I know that is how most of us were as children. Day by day and bit by bit, we bought into the rules of the machine and we lost the enthusiasm of youth.

I am sorry, but sometimes we just need to walk through the void or the unknown in order to get to our dreams. There are not promises. I have spent endless hours getting an education on the things I am passionate about or interested in. It is important to enjoy the process.

Furthermore, it is not energetically beneficial to get angry with the machine or drum up conspiracy theories. When we live a soul driven life there is not one minute for despair lest we miss another amazing insight or opportunity. Develop a healthy attitude toward money and people who have it. If you don't do this you will incur self karma. We live in an incredibly abundant world.

Each person has to take into account their own personality and circumstances. We all have our tolerance levels and issues we are working through. If you have to compromise something temporarily in order to pursue your dreams, there is nothing wrong with that. I have a friend who tapped into a small portion of the equity on her home to bolster a marketing effort for a children's book she wrote. She has been very successful and has had the money returned to her manifold. At the same time, someone else may feel trepidation over tapping into their equity. I have seen people tap into their equity and end up losing it on a business venture. Hopefully your inner guidance will lead you correctly.

You may have to work on yourself to become less rigid about your presets in order to live the life of your dreams. I promise you that complete rigidity will not get you anywhere but you need to determine your own pace. Naturally, always check in with your soul to get an answer on what it is you should soften up on or change.

Remember, what we fear will keep coming up over and over again. Once we deal with the fear, the issue vanishes.

I have seen many become terminally ill and die with plenty of money in the bank. The number one cure for all illnesses is to live with joy. There is no reason to trade health for money or material goods. You know the old saying – you can't take it with you. Seriously, if you are not feeling healthy, don't let a job kill you. I have done it and I have had to start over a few times. No matter what, if you have your health and clarity you can always begin again. The Universe will forgive us our mistakes as long as we do.

Other than a move toward more self-employment, I see more employee owned companies and profit sharing. With so many people waking up and taking back their power, this will be the only way that quality people are going to be willing to work for another entity.

Chapter Nine

A New World Awaits in the Unified Field

A Course in Miracles says that our world is a dysfunction and a clashing of egos. It is not good or bad. The dysfunctional realm is temporary and it is caused by karma or separation from God. The unified field (aka the vortex or the creative field) is a level of consciousness where all is well. This realm is omnipresent and eternal. One may exist in either, but not both at the same time – although there is a slight grey area on the outskirts of each realm. ACIM calls this level confusion. This separation may also be viewed as the separation of the head and the heart of humanity.

The traits of the lower self keep us separate from others and the traits of the higher self connect us with others in an authentic and harmonious fashion.

In a spiritual context, the ego creates a separate identity based on past imprinting and patterning and it can result in any variety of dispositions. The outcomes are limitless and therefore it is impossible to reach agreement when confronted with two or more separately evolving egos. The soul is part of the greater whole of humanity, which is also part of God and designed by God. For this reason many spiritualists say we are all one. This may sound like spiritualists are throwing a bunch of daisies through the air, but it is actually very challenging and humbling to drop ones ego in order to reach a place of harmony with others where life and relationships have the potential to be win/win.

It can be difficult to know if one is alignment or out of alignment and furthermore, alignment is not reached through behavior; it is achieved only by adjusting one's vibration. The nomenclature for raising our vibration consists largely of becoming the embodiment of Love, which is the fabric of higher consciousness.

Anybody who gets on a high horse and starts shaming other people is not aligned. The true higher self is much more insightful than that.

I realize that this concept is tricky. One may only understand this concept by experiencing it. You just have to try these concepts out and see what happens. Overall, aligning with the authentic self is imperative to being aligned with the unified field, but there are general characteristics that apply to all people.

I recall when I decided to focus only on feeling good before I began my day. I noticed that I would encounter other individuals during that day who were also in a good feeling place. On the contrary if I left the house feeling frustrated about something (whether or not the frustration was justified), I would encounter other disenchanted people. Most of us have experienced this concept. If you have not, I suggest you try it out and observe the results. We entrain our day by the energy we put out.

Deciding how to feel during your typical day is relatively easy compared to maintaining that alignment in more difficult circumstances. The issues that we face as a group are being purged at this time and the clashing of egos has caused polarization. Polarization is where the egos have pulled strongly in the direction of their perception and special viewpoint until there is extreme tension between the parties. Does this sound like the two major political parties in the 2016 election? Look around and you will see this same polarization playing out in many more aspects of society.

The concept of different wavelengths is not new, but it has become critical as the diverse energies are beginning to cluster even tighter as the years march on. We are vibrating into segments and groupings through law of attraction, much like the planets and galaxies have over millennia.

We cannot coerce others into alignment. Others have to be taking responsibility for their alignment consciously or subconsciously. Alignment is the stronger force in any energy system, so our being in alignment pulls others into alignment unless they are strongly resistant. ACIM alludes to this. We can usually tell how well we are aligned based on the alignment of those we encounter.

The list of characteristics that keep us aligned are:

Being in a high vibration – the embodiment of Love.
Having healed our past.
Being in the moment and keeping our soul in our body (grounding)
Trusting and taking inspired action.
Trusting everything we need will come to us and we don't have to fight or be aggressive.
Breathing in and breathing out of oxygen and spirit – give and receive in equal measure.
Staying connected to our spirit through our feeling center.
Knowing and trusting our gifts and insights
Being open to new information and experiences.

The primary reason we want to align with our soul and the unified field is so we may become our highest potential and make our best contribution while achieving greater states of inner peace and health. Our secondary reason for alignment is to bring others into that place. Our alignment has tremendous energetic potential for all of humanity because we are all connected. That's why "Be the Change" has become such a popular phrase.

At the most basic level you are Love. You are one with God and you are one with humanity. Your personality and your passions and gifts are the things that propel you and allow you to be a co-creator in this Universe.

I asked God, where may I find you?
I need you to show me the way.
I stilled my mind and listened
to what God had to say:

"I am the wind; I am calling
I am the sun that lights the day
I am crystal raindrops falling
When the sky is hazy grey
I am the answer to your questions
Your shelter in a storm
A gentle hand to guide you
A light that's clear and warm
I know your dreams and visions
I placed them there you see
For I am you
And you are me
Just follow your heart
And there I'll be"

Alana Kay

Websites
www.alanakay.com
www.violetphoenixpublishing.com

Other books by Alana Kay:

144,000 Points of Light: The Resurrection of the Legions of Archangel Michael

Heaven is Here: Our Ascent into the Fifth Dimension

Christ Consciousness Through the Twelve Aspects of Spiritual Love

How to Receive a High Quality Intuitive Reading

Intuition 101

Journal Space

www.ingramcontent.com/pod-product-compliance
Lightning Source LLC
Chambersburg PA
CBHW072017040426
42447CB00009B/1658